The Inspiring Life of
ITZHAK PERLMAN

Other Books by Carol Behrman:

Catch a Dancing Star (Dillon)
California Summer (Weekly Reader Books)
Stranger in my Heart (Weekly Reader Books)
The Wrong Kind (Weekly Reader Books)
Ghost in the Garden (Weekly Reader Books)
Old Enough to Dream (Weekly Reader Books)
The Christmas Orphan (Weekly Reader Books)
Friendship Blues (Weekly Reader Books)
Wendy's Choice (Weekly Reader Books)
Erica for President (Weekly Reader Books)
Wanted: One New Dad (Weekly Reader Books)
There's Only One You (Review & Herald)
The Remarkable Writing Machine (Julian Messner)
Become Your Own Ideal (Review & Herald)
Miss Dr. Lucy (Review & Herald)
Roberto Clemente (Globe Books)

Fiddler to the World

The Inspiring Life of
ITZHAK PERLMAN

Carol H. Behrman

SHOE TREE PRESS
WHITE HALL, VIRGINIA

Published by Shoe Tree Press, an imprint of
Betterway Publications, Inc.
P.O. Box 219
Crozet, VA 22932
(804) 823-5661

Cover design by Rick Britton
Cover photograph courtesy of Music Division,
NY Public Library for the Performing Arts,
Astor, Lenox & Tilden Foundations
Typography by Park Lane Associates

Copyright © 1992 by Carol H. Behrman

All rights reserved. No part of this book may be reproduced by any means, except by a reviewer who wishes to quote brief excerpts in connection with a review in a magazine or newspaper.

Library of Congress Cataloging-in-Publication Data

Behrman, Carol H.
    Fiddler to the world : the inspiring life of Itzhak Perlman / Carol H. Behrman.
       p. cm.
    Includes bibliographical references and index.
    Summary: Presents the life of the talented violinist whose bout with polio left him disabled but still determined to pursue his love of music and the violin.
    ISBN 1-55870-238-5 : $5.95
    1. Perlman, Itzhak, 1945- --Juvenile literature. 2. Violinists- -Biography--Juvenile literature. [1. Perlman, Itzhak, 1945- . 2. Violinists. 3. Musicians. 4. Physically handicapped.] I. Title.
ML3930.P45B4 1992
787.2'092--dc20
    [B]   91-43109
                                                                  CIP
                                                                  MN AC

Printed in the United States of America
0 9 8 7 6 5 4 3 2 1

*For Patrick and Luke
who are special and unique.*

ACKNOWLEDGMENTS

I would like to express my appreciation to the many people who assisted with the research for this book. A special thank-you to my writers' group for their help and encouragement, and to Isaac Stern, a great artist and wonderful human being, for his generosity in freely sharing his time and memories.

CONTENTS

	Introduction	11
1.	A Birth in the Holy Land	15
2.	The Battle with Polio	27
3.	Introduction to the Violin	35
4.	Childhood in Tel Aviv	45
5.	Coming to America	53
6.	A Carnegie Hall Debut	65
7.	Success in Career and Romance	79
8.	Expanding His Musical Horizons	89
9.	His Personal Life	103
10.	A Spokesman for the Disabled	113
	Bibliography	123
	Index	125

INTRODUCTION

Metal leg braces, crutches, a wheelchair — this is not the usual equipment carried onstage by a performer. Most entertainers, no matter how enthusiastic and extroverted, would want to run and hide. They would probably abandon any career in which they would be forced to display a crippling disability in the glare of the public eye.

Not so Itzhak Perlman! This performer brings something additional onto the stage that eclipses the paraphernalia of his handicap. His violin. When Perlman draws the bow across the strings of his Stradivarius, the sounds he brings forth rise above the details of their surroundings. The warmth and purity of his music unite audience and performer in a joyful celebration of the human soul that transcends physical limitations.

Itzhak Perlman's lower limbs are completely paralyzed. Incredible though it may seem, this disability is not something that occurred in maturity after the violinist had already begun his musical career. His disability is the result of a childhood disease. Itzhak Perlman was born in Israel. His father was a barber in the city of Tel Aviv. When he was only four years old, Itzhak contracted polio. After many months of convalescence, the child recovered from the illness but was left with permanent paralysis. Even so, the young Perlman saw no reason why he should not study the violin. It made no difference to him that the violin is one of the most difficult musical instruments to master. The enormous amount of physical and mental concentration and the dexterity and long hours of practice required are well beyond the capacity of most people even without a disability. Itzhak insisted, however, that the violin was for him. Fortunately, his supportive parents agreed and saw to it that Itzhak received lessons at the Music Academy in Tel Aviv.

From that time onward, Itzhak Perlman never wavered in his determination to pursue a musical career. He never acknowledged that his disability was in any way a handicap to his ambition. He practiced harder and longer than anyone else and, at the age of twelve and a half, he traveled to the United States, appeared on the Ed Sullivan television show, and took part in a three-month tour of gifted young musicians called "The Ed Sullivan Caravan of Stars."

The teenage violinist remained in America to continue his studies. He was accepted as a pupil by Ivan Galamian, a renowned teacher. In 1963, at the age of seventeen, Perlman made his concert debut at Carnegie Hall in New York. Since then, he has worked steadily and tirelessly, appearing at concert halls all over the world and making numerous recordings. Through the years, he kept on perfecting his technique until he became recognized as one of the outstanding violinists of the twentieth century. "Listening to him play," wrote one critic, "produced joy on every level—technical, musical and above all the human." Perlman's playing has been described as having a "joy" and a "bounce" that amaze even his colleagues. The same has been said of his personality—cheerful, warm, and enthusiastic.

The story of Itzhak Perlman's life is the tale of the journey of a polio-stricken little boy to become a man who has mastered not only his craft but his life as well. He ignored and rose above a disability that could have darkened all the years of his existence. By choosing the path of hope and acceptance, he has been able to share his love of music with millions of others throughout the world. The details of that difficult journey have not always been as painless and smooth as Itzhak Perlman's cheerful, uncomplaining attitude would suggest.

Chapter One

A BIRTH IN THE HOLY LAND

Some years stand out in history as being exceptionally eventful. Nineteen hundred and forty-five was such a year. It saw the end of World War II, a conflict in which the forces of destruction had come frighteningly close to plunging the world into a new Dark Age. In April 1945 Germany surrendered to the Allied powers. Adolf Hitler's dreams of world domination for his Third Reich were crushed forever. Millions of people who had been enslaved were liberated by the victorious Allies. The curtain of secrecy that had surrounded the Holocaust was ripped away, and the world was able to see for the first time the full extent of Nazi barbarity. Later that same year, the nuclear age was born when the United States Air Force dropped the atomic bomb on Hiroshima and Nagasaki. Japan, Germany's partner in conquest, surrendered in August, bringing this deadliest of all wars to a final close. By anyone's definition, this was, indeed, a landmark year.

Another event occurred in 1945. It was certainly not of the magnitude of war and peace, and it was not even noticed at the time except by those few who were personally involved. On the thirty-first of August, a little boy was born in the city of Tel Aviv, in the land of

Palestine, to Chaim and Shoshana Perlman. The proud parents were delighted with their baby. It was a special thrill to have brought a child into the world on the holy soil of *eretz Israel*, the promised land of their forefathers. That, in itself, was enough of a blessing and a small, personal affair. How could they have known that their child had a unique destiny and would one day bring pleasure and joy to music lovers around the globe?

Both Chaim and Shoshana were immigrants from Poland. In the 1930s they had each fled from the poverty, persecution, and pogroms in the land of their birth and from the Nazi horror that was already beginning to threaten the Jews of Europe. They were inspired by stories about a progressive new nation that was being created in the ancient Jewish homeland of Palestine. Chaim, from his village, and Shoshana, from hers, made the long, difficult journey to Palestine. Here, together with pioneers from around the world, they struggled and toiled on the barren, neglected soil to make it fertile and productive. These pioneers planted trees. They constructed irrigation ditches to provide water for the parched, arid land. They planted and built, sweated and strained. They erected clean, beautiful new cities. And they dreamed of reestablishing their ancient homeland and making it once again the biblical "land of milk and honey." It would be a place where Jews could live free, where they could hold up their heads proudly, and where they could be released from the fear of discrimination and persecution.

Chaim and Shoshana had left Europe just in time. The Nazi tentacles were beginning to reach ominously across the German border into Poland. In 1939, Nazi armies goose-stepped into Poland, crushing all resistance and enslaving the population. Those freedom-fighters who opposed the new tyranny were shot or deported, together with the Jewish citizens of Poland, to so-called "work camps." These evil prisons were, in reality, death centers. Together with six million other martyrs, Chaim's and Shoshana's families and friends disappeared into the extermination camps. In Auschwitz, Buchenwald, and other places of degradation and horror they suffered and died.

Chaim and Shoshana came from different towns in Poland. They had not known each other in the old country. Their meeting took place in Palestine. Here on the soil where their ancestors had walked in ancient days, they met, fell in love, and were married.

For a few years, the newlyweds lived and worked on a *kibbutz*. Many of these new-type farms had recently been established around Palestine by Jewish settlers. A kibbutz was a communal farm. All the land was owned in common by the people who lived and worked there. Each of the residents had equal responsibilities and equal rights in the work, organization, and government of the settlement. This cooperative way of farming proved to be extremely successful in Palestine. Working together, shoulder-to-shoulder, the pioneers were able to improve the soil through irrigation and modern farming methods, thus making their exertions profitable for all. Slowly and with great effort, they began to transform into rich, productive farms land that had grown barren through centuries of neglect.

For a while Chaim and Shoshana were happy living and working in the kibbutz. In that place, there was a wonderful sense of being involved in the creation of a new land and of sharing in an exciting, idealistic way of life. But neither Chaim nor Shoshana were farmers at heart, and after a while they began to yearn for city life. Eventually, they left the kibbutz and moved to the nearby city of Tel Aviv, where Chaim opened a barber shop.

Unlike many communities in this ancient land that had so many roots in the past, Tel Aviv was a fairly new city. It had been founded in the early part of the century as a suburb of the old town of Jaffa. The ancient city of Jaffa has laid claim to being the oldest port in the world. Some traditions hold that it was founded far back in biblical days by the son of Noah. The Bible also relates that it was from Jaffa that Jonah set sail upon the journey that would end with him inside the belly of a whale.

In 1909 a new suburb was constructed upon a cluster of sand dunes in the desert north of Jaffa. The new town was called Tel Aviv (The Hill of Spring), based upon a traditional name for these dunes, the origin of which was lost in antiquity. No one, not even the founders with their unbridled enthusiasm, ever dreamed that one day this tiny suburb would grow to become one of the three largest cities in the land of Israel. Indeed, in 1909 the concept of a Jewish nation was itself merely the vision of a few idealists. Only 2000 people were living in Tel Aviv in 1918 at the end of the First World War. By the time the Perlmans moved there, the population had grown to 165,000. After the Second World War, the expansion continued at an even more frantic rate. Since that time, the city has grown even more rapidly. It is now Israel's busiest city, with more than a million people in the metropolitan area and still growing.

In 1945 Tel Aviv was a bustling center of commerce, trade, and the arts. It was an original and unique city in a stirring new land that many people were already daring to think of as the nation of Israel. The atmosphere was one of enthusiasm, boundless energy, and unlimited hope for the future. The world was beginning to emerge from a period of gloom and fear into one of joy and optimism. World War II was ending

Street scenes in Tel Aviv. (Photos courtesy of J. & A. Colbert.)

with the defeat of the Axis powers. Those countries that had been enslaved under the Nazi yoke were now being freed. It was a time and a place filled with optimism, excitement, and unlimited dreams. This was where and when the first and only child of Chaim and Shoshana Perlman made his entrance into the world, on August 31, 1945. They gave him the name Itzhak, which is Hebrew for Isaac.

The proud parents could not have been happier. Their baby was healthy and beautiful. And it was a boy who would carry on the Perlman name, though Chaim and Shoshana could have no idea to what heights their newborn child would lift that name. Joyfully, the family celebrated the infant's *bris* (a party and blessing surrounding the rite of circumcision) with friends and brought their carefully-swaddled baby home to their small, walk-up apartment on a busy street in Tel Aviv. As Itzhak Perlman himself would later describe his first home: "The window had a wonderful view of the traffic, and the apartment was so small that the moment you opened the door, you were at the window."

Tiny though it was, the Perlmans, now a family of three, were blissfully happy in their nest. Itzhak's first four years there were as sunny and cloudless as the blue Mediterranean sky that warmed the streets of his native city. Chaim Perlman's barber shop thrived, in part thanks to newcomers from other parts of Israel and around the world who swelled Tel Aviv's population daily. Shoshana tended her baby with care and devotion and made friends with other mothers in the neighborhood. She kept their little home spotlessly clean and scrupulously *kosher* (in accordance with the Jewish dietary laws) and pursued her cultural interests, which were varied.

Both parents were intensely fond of classical music. The radio in the Perlman apartment was put into service frequently, filling the air with the sounds of the great symphonies and composers. Chaim and Shoshana had a special fondness for opera and they loved to hum melodies from operas such as *Carmen*, *La Traviata*, and others. They were proud and delighted when Itzhak, at two and a half, was able to sing out portions of operatic arias he had heard on the radio.

When he was three years old, Itzhak one day came upon his parents listening to a recording by the renowned violinist, Jascha Heifetz. The boy listened intently to the sweet melodic strains that were emanating from the radio. He had a rapt expression on his face. Shortly after that, Itzhak demanded a violin of his own. His proud father immediately rushed out and purchased an inexpensive toy violin for his little son, the "prodigy."

Itzhak fully expected to be able to play like Heifetz immediately. What a disappointment it was to discover that he was not quite ready to become a prodigy. He tried to play his little instrument, but when it turned out that he could not create sounds that even remotely resembled what he had heard from the bow of the maestro, he impatiently discarded his new toy. "I'm too young to play," he told his parents in disgust. He did not, however, give up his enjoyment of this stringed instrument, but continued to listen to it on the radio with interest and delight. As a grown man, he later admitted that he could not recall a time in his life when he did not want to play the violin.

In May of 1948, the Jewish people in Palestine fought and won a war of independence. Israel became a nation. This was affirmed by the rest of the world later that year. In November, the United Nations passed a resolution recognizing the existence of the state of Israel. The Perlmans, along with their fellow citizens, rejoiced that their ancient people, so long oppressed, now had a homeland of their own.

The following year, when Itzhak was four, a terrible plague descended upon the land. Israel was struck by a severe and deadly epidemic of polio.

Poliomyelitis! Just the name of this fearful, crippling disease was enough to strike terror into the hearts of the parents of Tel Aviv, just as it had for centuries in every part of the world where it had struck. Sometimes referred to as infantile paralysis, epidemics had been known since ancient times. Egyptian artifacts have been dug up that point to the possibility that infantile paralysis had occurred there as far back as 1500 B.C. No records of polio epidemics were kept, however, until 1835, when the disease appeared in the village of Worksop, England. Doctors studied this epidemic and others of a similar nature that occurred in various parts of the world. They soon began to associate the paralysis with mysterious damage to the spinal cords of children who had been infected with this terrible illness. No treatment seemed to be effective, and more and more epidemics began to spread, like a black plague, across the globe. In the late 1800s one hundred and thirty-two children were stricken in the Otter Creek valley of Vermont. Eighteen of them died. Thereafter, the incidence and severity of epidemics of polio rose steadily around the world.

Although doctors and researchers studied this disease for many years, it wasn't until 1955 that Dr. Jonas Salk in the United States succeeded in developing a vaccine that would immunize children against polio. That discovery was a turning point in the fight against poliomyelitis. Some time after Jonas Salk's breakthrough discovery, Dr. Albert Sabin, another American researcher, perfected a different kind of polio vaccine. Sabin's vaccine could be administered orally. Today, wherever vaccination programs have

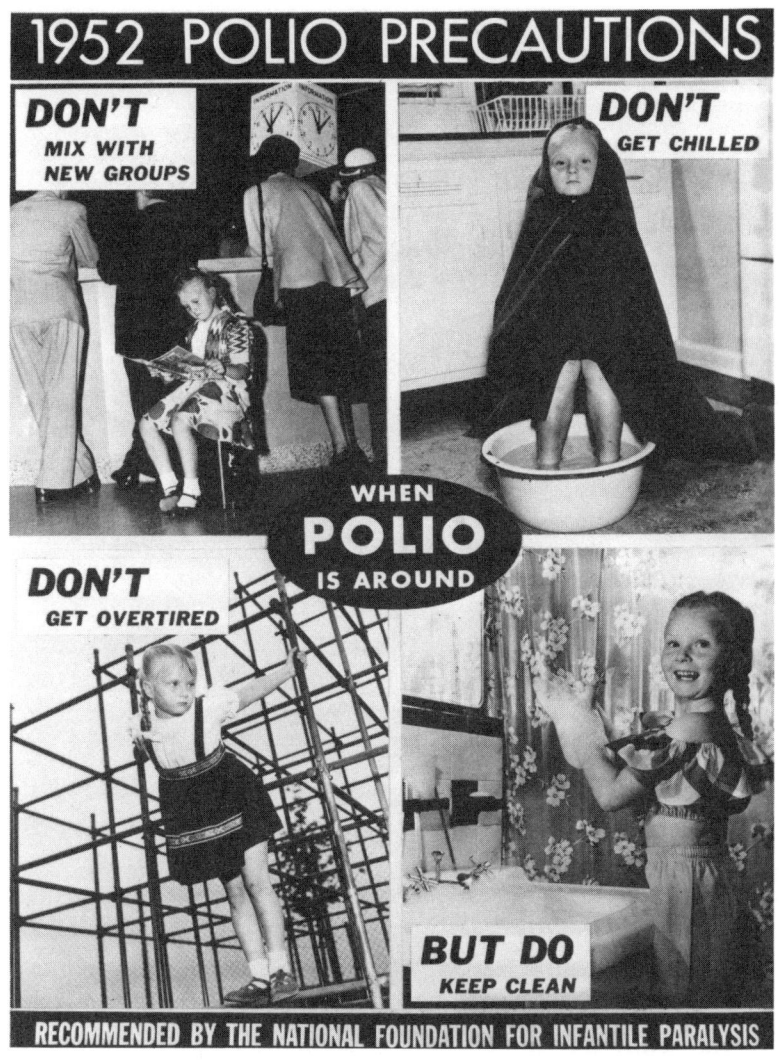

Before the development of a polio vaccine, posters such as this were used in prevention campaigns. (Photo courtesy of March of Dimes Birth Defects Foundation.)

been put into effect using either the Salk or Sabin vaccines, infantile paralysis has been almost totally eliminated.

In 1949 when the epidemic hit Israel, there was nothing that parents could do to protect their children. They were helpless to do more than worry and watch anxiously for signs of infection. There was hardly a mother or father in the city of Tel Aviv who was not well-informed about the symptoms of polio. The dreaded disease often began deceptively, with mild, flu-like aches and pains. Many a child with nothing more serious than a cold was kept in bed and fretted over for days. If it was polio, however, these symptoms would grow steadily worse, and might be followed by high fever, unbearable headaches, and stiffness and pain in the back and neck. If the virus continued to spread, it could pass from the bloodstream into the central nervous system. Once the nerve cells became infected, paralysis of the legs, the arms, and sometimes even the chest would then develop quickly along with the fever.

After the acute stage of the disease, with its raging fever, delirium, and excruciating pain, ran its course, and the deadly virus finally stopped its assault against the helpless young body, some children would be fortunate enough to recover completely. Others would be paralyzed for life. Still others, unfortunately, would die. It was impossible for doctors to predict the outcome in individual cases. Like the distraught parents, the medical experts could do little more than wait and hope.

Panic spread through Tel Aviv and the surrounding area like a five-alarm fire. Nervous families kept their children indoors and away from crowds. When, despite all the Perlmans' precautions, four-year-old Itzhak became ill, Chaim and Shoshana immediately called their doctor. He examined the boy and, with a worried frown, informed the Perlmans that they would have to bring their stricken child to the hospital. With great fear and apprehension, the terrified parents followed the physician's instructions.

The hospital was crowded with sick children. An atmosphere of doom hung over its sterile corridors. There, while the desperate parents hovered anxiously over their boy's limp and pallid body, Itzhak lay for many days, hanging in an eerie limbo between life and death. His terrified mother and father hovered nearby, anguished by their helplessness to do anything for their suffering child.

Chapter Two

THE BATTLE WITH POLIO

A week after the polio struck, the doctor came out to the waiting room to find the haggard parents.

"The crisis has passed."

The Perlmans looked up as the doctor spoke. They were worn out and bleary-eyed from days and nights without sleep.

"Itzhak? Our boy?"

The doctor smiled. "He's okay."

"And we can take him home?"

The doctor nodded.

Chaim and Shoshana smiled, hugged each other, and shook the doctor's hand gratefully. Chaim went in to get his son. As soon as he saw Itzhak, he realized, with a sinking feeling, that he had misunderstood the meaning of what the doctor had told him. When the doctor had said that the boy was "okay," he had only meant that Itzhak was still alive.

But he was a pathetic sight. The four-year-old boy lay inert like a feeble little rag doll. He was unable to move his arms or his legs. All of his limbs were completely paralyzed. The fever was gone. The invading virus had halted its deadly assault on the child's body short of killing him. Itzhak was still alive. But in what a helpless condition! And his parents could not help but wonder, with a stab of pain, what sort of life might lie ahead for this stricken little boy.

Sadly, Chaim gathered his child into his arms. He and Shoshana brought Itzhak home.

Once the initial shock of seeing their son paralyzed had worn off, the Perlmans were gradually able to overcome that petrifying sense of doom and despair. They were thankful that Itzhak was, at least, alive. They had their child home with them. He still had his mind, his intelligence, and his wonderful spirit. Despite all he had been through, the four-year-old boy found it possible to be cheerful and hopeful.

Chaim and Shoshana decided then and there that, no matter how hard the struggle, they would raise their son as a normal child. They would support and guide him, and make him feel like a human being. "We did everything," Chaim Perlman said, "not to make Itzhak feel handicapped."

It wasn't easy. The polio virus had infected the motor neurons of the spinal cord and deadened the nerves that affected Itzhak's arms and legs. The child had no movement or sensation in these limbs. He was helpless to do anything for himself.

There is a prescribed course of treatment for paralysis that has occurred as a result of polio. In the 1930s an Australian nurse, Sister Elizabeth Kenny (nurses are called "sisters" in Australia), had developed a new technique for combatting the paralysis associated with polio. Her method involved exercise, manipulation of affected limbs, and specialized stimulation of the muscle systems involved. As time went on, other physicians and therapists began to use and expand upon Sister Kenny's theories. There have been many positive results and also many disappointments with this method. The course of treatment usually begins with the

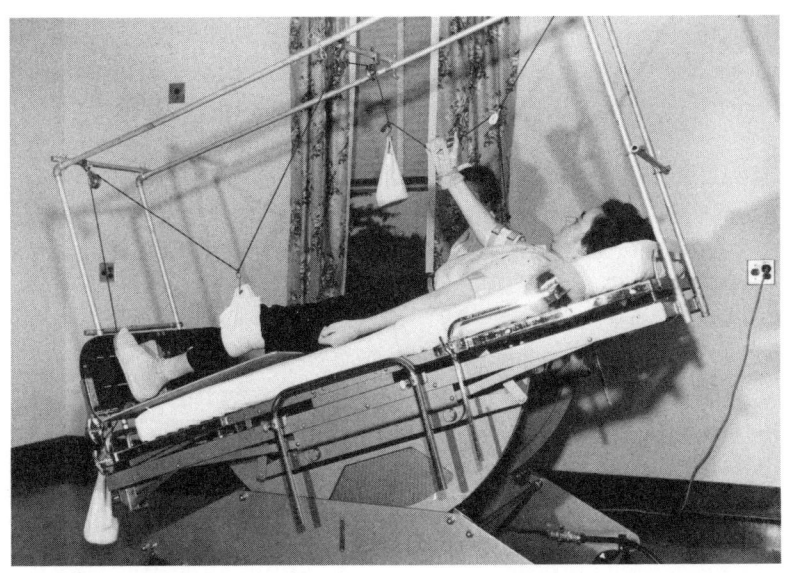

A "rocking bed" was sometimes used in the treatment of paralysis. (Photo courtesy of March of Dimes Birth Defects Foundation.)

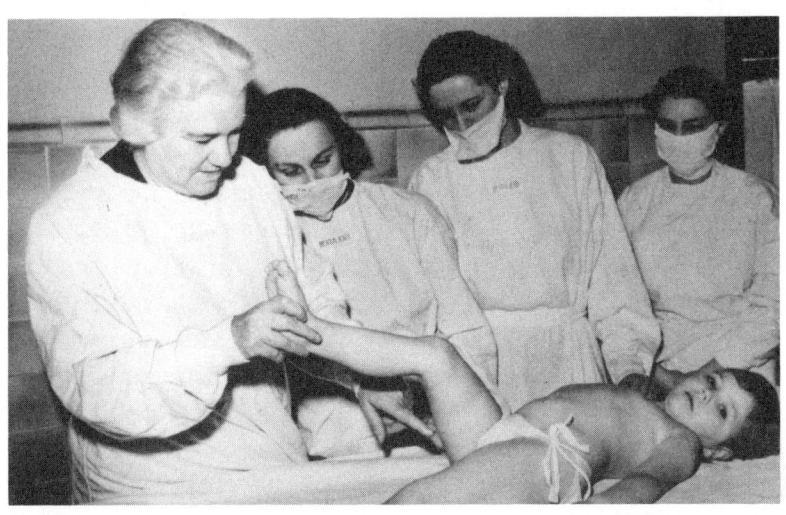

Sister Elizabeth Kenny, an Australian nurse, developed techniques for treating polio victims. (Photo courtesy of Sister Kenny Institute.)

application of moist, hot packs over the affected muscles. Then the limbs receive regular massage and stimulation. At first, these exercises are gentle. The patient is passive. He can do nothing for himself. His therapist must do all the work — rubbing the paralyzed areas, bending them, moving them up and down. Though the prognosis for complete cure is often discouragingly dim, it is important that the affected limbs be exercised as much as possible if there is to be any hope at all for improvement.

After a while, the exercises are strengthened and increased. Whenever possible, the patient is urged to attempt to do as much as he can for himself. Warm baths and underwater therapy in a pool are used to stimulate weakened tissues. This is an important part of the treatment. It promotes healing and aids in developing any muscles that are capable of being revived.

Thus, the road back to life began for four-year-old Itzhak Perlman. It was a constant struggle against pain, frustration, and failure. Many times the patient was tempted to give up what seemed like a hopeless struggle. Even at this young age, however, it was evident that this child was not a quitter. The boy did everything he was told to do, and he did it as cheerfully as possible under difficult circumstances. He cooperated in every way that he could. His bright, optimistic outlook was a beacon for those who worked with him. At times, it even helped his parents surmount their own moments of doubt and despair.

Eventually, after much tedious, difficult, and exhausting therapy, it was noted that some feeling and movement had begun to return to the boy's arms and hands. One can only imagine the joy and celebration this hopeful event brought to the Perlman household. It was, however, only a beginning. Many more months of constant treatment and exercise were necessary before real strength came back to Itzhak's arms and hands.

Sadly, the same was not true for his legs. Despite faithful and continuous work by his parents and therapists, and by the boy himself, Itzhak's legs remained paralyzed. Although the prospect of permanent disability was hard for the parents to accept, it soon became evident that the only way Itzhak would ever be able to walk was with the assistance of braces and crutches.

Mastering these clunky mechanical aids was a difficult and awkward procedure. Itzhak had to learn how to navigate on legs from which all feeling had departed and that were weighted down by heavy metal cages. Even with hard work and absolute concentration, moving paralyzed limbs within a metal prison often seemed like an impossible goal. It took many, many hours of instruction and often frustrating practice before the boy succeeded in taking a few tentative steps with the support of these clumsy, artificial devices.

The first year after Itzhak's illness was discouraging and difficult for the Perlman family. Their energies were concentrated on the illness and its awful aftermath. Almost all their time and effort was centered around the boy and his disability. Their lives were defined by the never-ending demands of each day, involving treatment rooms, hospitals, therapists, and Itzhak's constant, pressing needs.

Eventually, however, the family began to regain a semblance of normal life. As time went on, Itzhak's determined and optimistic spirit glowed more and more brightly. As Itzhak grew more proficient with his braces and crutches and gradually became able to do some things for himself, the Perlmans found the time and energy to begin thinking about the future. As they contemplated the years that lay ahead, Chaim and Shoshana became more and more determined to bring up their child in a way that emphasized not his handicap but his talents and capabilities. They would not lose their boy to a disability!

Itzhak had never lost his interest in the violin that had first surfaced when he was a toddler. If anything, his months of inactivity had intensified his feelings for music. Tel Aviv in the late 1940s was a perfect background for nurturing an emerging music-lover. Although new and raw as cities go, the city of Tel Aviv was already becoming a center of culture. While Itzhak Perlman was making his slow, tortuous recovery from polio, the leaders of Tel Aviv were already planning a magnificent cultural center to extend over an area of six acres. When it was finally completed in 1957, the Cultural Center of Tel Aviv would include a National Theatre, or "Habimah," the Helena Rubinstein Museum of Arts, and the Frederic R. Mann Auditorium, a concert hall with 2700 seats that would provide a home for Israel's Philharmonic Orchestra.

Many of the city's inhabitants, like the Perlmans themselves, were émigrés from Europe. They brought with them the appreciation of music, art, and drama that had flourished in their native lands. They sought to reproduce these cultural activities here in their new homeland of Israel. Many small amateur and professional orchestras and bands flourished in various parts of the city. Renowned musicians came to perform in Tel Aviv. Music, especially classical music, was in the air, on the radio, along the colorful, bustling streets, and in the homes of the residents. Itzhak, whose movements were impeded by his illness and by his handicaps, was not restricted in his enjoyment of music.

About a year after the polio had first struck him down, Itzhak again asked his parents for a violin. Chaim and Shoshana were delighted to oblige. They were in agreement that a musical interest would be good for the boy. It would be something to occupy his mind and his spirit and would offer him a stimulating challenge. It would enable him to learn a rewarding skill that did not depend on the use of his legs. And, if nothing else, it was good physical therapy. Playing an instrument such as the violin would certainly provide excellent exercise for strengthening his arms and upper body.

As for Itzhak himself, young as he was, he had never really given up his ambition to play like his idol, the violin virtuoso Jascha Heifetz. Itzhak had no way of knowing, of course, what a difficult task he was setting for himself. Of all the instruments that he might have chosen, the violin was one of the toughest and most challenging for any student, even one without a disability, to master. Nevertheless, Itzhak loved music, he adored the sound of the violin, and he was determined to learn how to play it.

Chapter Three

INTRODUCTION TO THE VIOLIN

Young people, more than many others, understand what a vital part music plays in their lives. It helps them to get in touch with their feelings and with themselves. It plugs them into the currents, ideas, and language of their generation. It brings pleasure, magic, and excitement into their day-by-day existence. If Itzhak Perlman had been brought up amid the pop culture of America in the 1990s, his love of music might have led him to an interest in playing a rock guitar or a synthesizer. In his time, place, and cultural environment, it was the classical violin that awoke and excited the boy's musical interests.

This impulse toward musical expression has been part of human societies since the beginning of time. Even primitive peoples used crude musical instruments as an important part of their cultures. The stone age tom-tom has its modern-day model in the rhythmic beat of the drum. The violin may also have had its origins back among unknown musicians of the ancient world. No one knows for sure when stringed instruments first made their appearance upon the scene. Some experts believe the earliest stringed instrument probably came into existence by accident thousands of years ago. A cave-dwelling hunter may have been surprised and delighted to notice the pleasing tones that came forth when he pulled at the cord of his hunting bow. Perhaps it reminded him of some soothing natural sound, like a tinkling waterfall. With a little imagination and dexterity, this prehistoric ancestor could have created the first silver-toned sound of strings to entertain his companions around a campfire.

A stringed instrument called the lyre was popular in ancient Greece and Rome. There, singing was often accompanied by plucking the strings of this instrument with the fingers or with a *plectrum*, a small piece of metal or wood that was used to pluck the strings. Old Celtic tribes in the British Isles, back in the mists of pre-history, used the other-worldly sounds of the harp to enhance the mystical sense of their religious rites.

The violin differs from the lyre, the harp, and other ancient instruments in many ways. Most important is the use of the bow in drawing it across the strings instead of plucking them with the fingers. The bow is the magic wand that gives the violin its distinctive depth of expression. By using a bow, the musician is able to draw sounds out to make them last longer, and he can increase or lower their tone, depth, and color. Thus, music can be created that has greater feeling, intensity, and range.

It is believed that a bow was first used in parts of Asia. The Persians had such an instrument, which was called a *rebab*. Arabians used a *rebeb*, also played with a bow. This became the *rebec* in medieval Europe, which later was transformed into the *fidel*, or *fidula*. This stringed instrument was played with a *fidelstyk*, an early kind of bow. Our modern-day word, *fiddle*, comes from this source.

All of these early forerunners to the violin, including the *fidel*, were made with only three strings. A

A 1709 Stradivarius. (Photo courtesy of Smithsonian Institute, from the Axelrod Quartet.)

fourth string was added by a brilliant but unknown innovator sometime during the sixteenth century, and that was when the modern violin was born.

It was during this period that the finest violin-makers the world has ever known appeared upon the scene. They all lived and worked in Italy, in and around the town of Cremona. The first great violin craftsman there was named Andreas Amati. He carefully trained his sons, Nicola, Antonio, and Hieronymus, to carry on his work. They were followed by Antonio Stradivari and Joseph Guarneri.

Amati. Stradivari. Guarneri. These are the legendary names in the world of the classical violin. During the sixteenth and seventeenth centuries, these highly-gifted artisans crafted musical instruments that have never been surpassed. Many other excellent violins have been produced since then, but none has ever equalled the beauty of appearance and sound that was created by Amati, Stradivari, and Guarneri. The secrets of these master violin-makers seem to have died with them. No one really knows how they created such perfect instruments. Modern violin-makers have tried all sorts of experiments. They have baked wood in ovens and even tried burying it in sand for years, all to no avail. The violins these specially-designed woods went into bore no resemblance to the products of the masters.

Fortunately, however, many of the violins the craftsmen of Cremona built are still in existence. These instruments are used and treasured by the professional musicians who have been lucky enough to obtain them. They have enormous value, both artistically and financially.

Nowadays, many violins are mass-produced. They are cut, shaped, and put together with the help of time-saving machines in modern, speed-oriented factories.

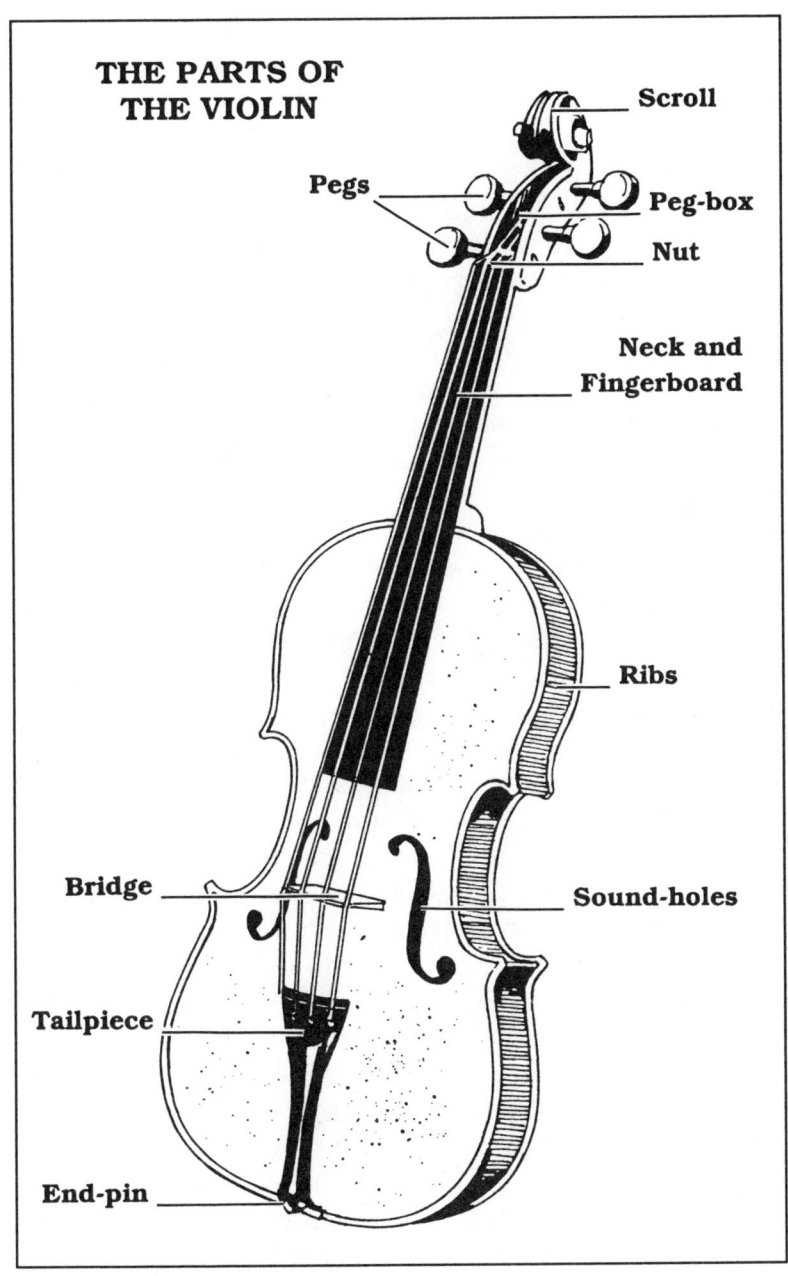

The parts of the violin.

These instruments can be manufactured cheaply. They are inexpensive. They offer an opportunity for violin ownership to people who may not be able to afford a more expensive one. They are also used extensively in public school music study programs. While limited in the quality of sound and music that they are capable of producing, these violins serve an important purpose, especially for beginning students.

There are, however, many individual violin-makers who still turn out superior handmade products. These artisans are scattered throughout the world. In their shops, they painstakingly craft hand-carved instruments in the manner of the great artisans of the past. Naturally, such individually crafted violins cost considerably more than their machine-made counterparts. The extra expense is, of course, well worth it for the serious music student. It is not difficult to identify these superior violins. They usually carry somewhere on the instrument the signature label of their makers, including the time and place of the violin's manufacture.

There is one modern violin-maker who claims to have discovered the long-lost secret of the master craftsmen of Cremona. He uses wood that is treated to make it more like the wood that once floated down river from the Italian Alps to the lagoons of Venice, and then brought to Cremona. These new violins also use a special varnish that is made with many finely-ground minerals. They can sell for as much as $15,000, but there is no evidence they can produce anywhere near the purity and clarity of tone that is possible with the great seventeenth-century instruments.

Have you ever seen a violin up close and examined the way it is made? The secret of its sweet, pleasing voice lies in its construction. The structure of the violin is simple, but it is cleverly designed to produce sounds that are beautiful and unique. The main part of the violin is a hollow, oval body. The top and bottom of this body are curved. Two sound holes are cut on either side of the bridge. These holes are f-shaped. A neck that contains the pegs is fixed to the upper part of the body. A fingerboard is then glued to the neck of the violin. Strings are stretched across this fingerboard.

The strings are made of gut, fine wire, or a combination of gut and wire. (Gut is a strong, sturdy cord that is made from animal intestines.) The strings are wound around tuning pegs at the end of the fingerboard. The pegs can be tightened or loosened to make the pitch on each string higher or lower. The heavier strings are lower-pitched than the finer ones. The strings run across the bridge and are attached to a tailpiece at the bottom of the instrument.

Although this structure seems fairly simple, the details of its construction are varied and complicated. It is these intricacies of craftsmanship, however, that determine the quality of sound that each individual instrument is capable of producing.

Through the ages, both musicians and ordinary people have enjoyed and appreciated the almost unearthly beauty of the music that this stringed instrument can bring forth. The violin, when played by a talented performer, can create sounds of such purity and sweetness that a listener sometimes feels as though his very soul has been pierced.

The problem is that this most beautiful and complex of instruments is also one of the most difficult to master. Anyone who has ever heard a beginning student trying to create even a moderately decent sound knows the painful, jarring, scratching noises that usually result. There are so many complicated fine points that the student must learn. For example, *vibrato* is the term that is given to how fast and widely the fingers vibrate on the fingerboard. This cannot really be taught. Success depends on the amount of concentrated practice the student is willing to put forth, and on his innate talent.

Itzhak Perlman himself has spoken about some of the many complex factors that are involved in playing his instrument. "You have to worry about whether to move the bow slowly or quickly," he says. "Is the bow absolutely straight? How hard do you want to press the bow against the strings? All this involves just the right hand. Then there is the left hand.... Just to get a decent sound can take years. And only then do you start thinking of the music and developing your distinctive style."

Besides this, there are the dangers provided by the instrument itself. The violin is so sensitive that its tone can be affected by the weather. In the middle of a performance, a string can, without warning, suddenly go flat, causing no end of problems for the performer. Even worse, a string can snap apart, bringing to awful reality a violinist's worst nightmare—standing on the stage holding an instrument from which dangles a useless, twanging string.

One professional violinist has described his instrument as "the most hellish invention ever conceived by man, a beautiful and treacherous work of art." Jascha Heifetz himself, one of the greatest violinists of all time, commented simply, but significantly, on the unpredictability and sensitivity of his precious violin by saying, "Treat her right and she'll treat you right." Heifetz also remarked that a concert violinist needed "the nerves of a bullfighter, the vitality of a woman who runs a night club, and the concentration of a Buddhist monk."

A tale is told about the legendary Italian violinist, Niccolo Paganini, who was born in 1782 and died in 1840. It is believed by many musical historians that

Paganini was the most accomplished violinist who ever lived, and that his incredible artistry and technical skill have never been equalled. There is a legend that Paganini, when young, made a pact with the devil and sold his soul for the privilege of becoming the greatest violinist of all time. This story was nurtured by Paganini himself. His appearance was gaunt and ghoulish and he lived a dissipated life that ruined his health. Most of all, however, there was his brilliant technique. It was said that he could bring forth sounds from his instrument that were impossible for any human being to achieve. How could this be accomplished, his contemporaries thought, without an unholy alliance with Satan? Their willingness to believe such a tale only illustrates the wide recognition, even then, that mastering the violin is a tough, often unachievable goal.

How difficult can it be to play this instrument? Here is the way that Franz Liszt, famed pianist and composer, described the problems of a violinist friend. "My God, what suffering, what despair, what torment in those four strings!"

This is the violin — the musical instrument that five-year-old Itzhak Perlman, permanently crippled by polio, set out to master. It may have seemed like an almost impossible task. There was one quality, however, that Itzhak Perlman possessed, even as a child, that was a formidable weapon in the conquest of this difficult instrument. That quality was persistence, a stubbornness in trying to attain a goal, and an ability to "stick to it."

This quality is one that appears to be shared by many handicapped people. Perhaps it is because they have been forced to face up to their condition. They can't ignore it, no matter how fervently they might wish that they could. Unlike others who can be turned away from success by minor complications and small defeats, handicapped people must confront failure many times. By doing so and continuing to struggle on despite those failures, they learn how to surmount and overcome them. Such people may refuse to admit that a goal may be unreachable for them. They continue to work, to try, to struggle until they achieve what they have set out to accomplish.

This insistence on reaching "the unreachable star" is a necessary ingredient for success no matter who the individual may be. For the handicapped, it is even more essential. Practical people will always be there to tell those who aspire to some high goal that it's impossible, that they don't have what it takes, that they weren't born into the right circumstances. Forget about it, they are advised.

There must have been those who told five-year-old Itzhak Perlman that a cripple shouldn't even consider trying to master a difficult instrument like the violin. "Try something easier," they probably said.

But the child was stubborn. He didn't listen to any such naysayers. The "impossible" seemed perfectly possible to him.

Chapter Four

CHILDHOOD IN TEL AVIV

"I had a fairly normal childhood," Itzhak Perlman once remarked, "considering two rather unusual elements. I had polio and walked with crutches, and I practiced the violin two to three hours a day." He also adds the information that, of the two, the violin was harder to explain at the time.

When four-year-old Itzhak was brought home from the hospital after his illness, the Perlmans were still living in their cramped, third-floor walk-up apartment near Chaim's barber shop. They found this setup too difficult to manage during the boy's convalescence. Also, Chaim and Shoshana feared that these living arrangements could impede Itzhak's ability to become independent eventually. They decided that the family would have to move. No sacrifice was too great when it came to the welfare of their child.

They found a first-floor apartment in a suburb of the city. The building in which the apartment was located was close to an elementary school. It was a perfect place to bring up a disabled child. Chaim's business posed the only problem. It would no longer be possible for him to commute to his barber shop in the city. Aside from other considerations, this daily trip would not have given Chaim enough time to be with Itzhak. The boy needed help now more than ever. He faced a long period of recuperation. Chaim had no wish to be an absentee father. He was determined to be there to lend his physical and emotional support as much as possible. The child needed both parents to guide him through his various therapies. Their strength could help the boy cope with the difficulties he was certain to encounter as he learned to adjust to his disability.

Chaim, who was always resourceful, was able to sell the barber shop in the city. The Perlmans then moved into their new apartment. Once there, Chaim solved the problem of how he would support his family. He purchased a small self-service laundry nearby. Chaim, Shoshana, and their son settled into their new home. Itzhak's intensive physical therapy continued. Slowly — very slowly — his arms and hands became stronger. After what seemed like an eternity, his upper body developed enough power to begin another painful struggle—learning to walk with the aid of braces and crutches.

Chaim and Shoshana were delighted to encourage the boy's interest in music. When Itzhak told his father, "Now, I want to learn to play the violin," Chaim went right out to the nearest music shop. This time, he purchased a real instrument, not a toy, for his son. Five-year-old Itzhak was not quite ready for a Stradivarius. In fact, at the time his parents were struggling financially and could not even afford to purchase a new violin. The instrument that the future prodigy played at the very beginning of his career was a used one. It cost Chaim Perlman the equivalent of six dollars.

The boy seized the violin with as much assurance as though he were already a full-fledged virtuoso. Even before beginning to take lessons, almost as if by instinct, Itzhak was somehow able to find the correct fingering and to bring forth some tentative sounds. It almost seemed as though he had been born into this lifetime already knowing how to play his chosen instrument. Everyone was amazed. Yet, even to a student with such extraordinary natural ability, the violin does not yield up its secrets easily. The tones that Itzhak managed to produce were excellent for a small person, five years of age. But the violin poses such difficulties for a beginner —even a gifted beginner like Itzhak—that the boy had to practice long and hard. Perlman later admitted that "it took me a year or two to get a good sound—I mean one that you could stand, a sound that would not make you want to throw things at me or run out of the house." Even a prodigy, it seems, must struggle. "People started to say I had a nice tone," Perlman recalled, "when I was about nine or ten."

Itzhak was enrolled for music lessons at the Tel Aviv Academy of Music. The Perlmans settled into a busy, but comfortable, routine that would be followed for many years. The parents worked hard. As much as possible, they reared their son in a normal, ordinary way, emphasizing his strengths instead of his disability. They encouraged him to become independent and to engage in as many activities as he could. Itzhak, just like all the other boys his age, attended the nearby elementary school. After school and on weekends, he played with his pals. (After he had put in his three hours of violin practice, of course.)

From an early age, Itzhak treated his disability with common sense and good humor. This communicated itself to other children. Like Itzhak himself, they came to accept his handicap as a part of their friend, as something that was just there. After all, one fellow might be painfully shy; another might be known for having an uncontrollable temper; another might be less clever than his companions. They were all individuals.

Itzhak just happened to be the one who needed crutches. Itzhak was even able to play soccer out in the street with the other kids. "I was the goalie," he later recalled. "With both my crutches and my legs, I could stop anything." This was just one example of the humorous, good-natured way the boy dealt with his paralysis. There was no self-pity demonstrated here, no off-putting attitude of "poor me." As a result, he was always popular and well-accepted.

Tel Aviv in the 1950s was an exciting place to be growing up. The new nation of Israel, only a few years old, was filled with an air of optimism and great expectations. Despite a constant threat of attack by their Arab neighbors, the Israelis continued to plant and build and dream of greatness for their fledgling nation.

The city of Tel Aviv was growing and spreading in a wild surge of building and expansion. By the mid 1950s it had become Israel's largest city. Its population, including the suburbs, was 400,000 and increasing almost daily. Factories, office buildings, and modern residential areas were being created with incredible speed.

Despite its rapid growth, Tel Aviv had not lost the atmosphere of culture instilled by its earliest settlers. The city's tree-bordered avenues were lined with bookstores and music shops. By 1957, Tel Aviv was the cultural center of Israel. It was the site of three major theaters. A magnificent new concert hall, the Frederic R. Mann Auditorium, had just been completed as a home for the Israeli Philharmonic Orchestra, and ground had been broken for a huge new university.

A child growing up in Tel Aviv had the advantage of contact with people who had come from all corners of the globe to settle there. Yemenite craftsmen mixed with the settlers from eastern Europe who had helped found the city. Jews from the ghettos of Morocco rubbed shoulders with doctors and scientists from Berlin's west end. And there were the young native Israelis, such as Itzhak himself. They were called *sabras* after a desert fruit that is tough on the outside but tender and sweet within. Native-born Israelis liked to think of this as a description of themselves.

One sabra, young Itzhak Perlman, was exactly the opposite. He was gentle, good-natured, and sweet on the outside. But the inner self of this physically-disabled child was as strong as rock—strong enough to overcome the handicaps a cruel disease had left with him.

In this throbbing, intensely-alive environment, the boy Itzhak studied, dreamed, grew, and played with the neighborhood children.

There were, of course, some things the other kids did that were denied Itzhak due to his handicap. That was okay with him, though, because it gave him more time to devote to playing his beloved violin. Most youngsters who take music lessons find it an unpleasant chore to practice. The hour is endured impatiently, with one eye upon the clock. Not Itzhak! This was what he preferred doing above all else.

It soon became evident to his teachers and his parents that the boy's abilities as a violinist were far above the ordinary. In fact, he more and more began to demonstrate a rare musical talent. At the Music Academy, he was awarded a scholarship by the America-Israel Cultural Foundation and was taken on as a pupil by Madame Rivka Goldcart, a highly sought-after teacher. Famous classical artists who visited the Tel Aviv Academy in those days were entranced with the curly-haired child who played while sitting down and smiled despite his braces and crutches.

Within a few years, the child was making appearances with the Ramat-Gan Orchestra of Tel Aviv and the Broadcasting Orchestra in Jerusalem. His training and the number of public appearances he made were somewhat rigorous, but he was not pushed as aggressively as might have been the case if the boy were not handicapped. Despite his obviously outsized talent, it was thought at first that Itzhak's disability would make a large-scale solo career impossible. Even though no one else pressured Itzhak, however, he could not ignore the pressures to excel that came from within himself. He worked long and conscientiously on the tedious scales and exercises that any serious student of music must contend with. He also put in the necessary effort to build up a small repertoire of violin solos that would have frightened off most children his age.

Itzhak gave his first solo recital when he was only ten years old. It was an unusual and impressive sight for concert-goers to see the little boy come onto the stage with a jaunty bounce, smiling broadly despite his obviously useless legs and the clumsy devices he had to use for support.

Unlike other violinists, he had to sit down when performing. Violin soloists prefer to stand erect when they are playing. In this way, they are able to bring the strength of their entire body behind the bow. Itzhak Perlman, of course, has always had to perform seated. Even as a youngster, however, he was somehow able to overcome that disadvantage. As soon as he began to play, the audience would find itself caught up in the power of the music he was able to produce. They would forget they were watching the performance of a crippled child, and they would only know that here was a remarkable student who was destined for greatness.

Chaim and Shoshana were proud of their son, not only because of his immense talent, but even more so because of the courageous way he had managed to overcome his disability. Many people, no matter how great their potential, might allow such a handicap to take over their lives and to place a limit on what they might achieve. No one would blame them. Such a reaction would be only human and natural. But Itzhak, though only a child, found the inner strength to accept what had happened to him and to go on from there to be the best that he could be.

When he grew up and looked back at his childhood, Itzhak would give much of the credit for his positive attitude to his parents. "They instinctively did things right," he would say. "They treated me in a natural way." Chaim and Shoshana provided their son with a healthy, uncomplaining background. They were totally committed to his well-being. They did everything possible to help him become independent. Certainly, their sensitive and intelligent parenting contributed to Itzhak's remarkable ability to rise above his handicap. There was something more, however—a will, a serenity, a light within the little boy that could not be snuffed out, not even by polio.

Word was getting around in the music world that there was an unusual young violin prodigy in Tel Aviv. Famous musicians such as Leonard Bernstein and Isaac Stern traveled to Israel to see him perform. Stern, who is considered by many music critics to be the foremost violinist of our time, was especially impressed by the virtuosity of the young violinist. Stern recalls that even at the age of ten or eleven, Itzhak's playing stood out. "It had a quality," Stern says, "that *demands* that you listen—doesn't ask permission."

Then, like the mysterious stranger who suddenly rides into town in classic films about the Old West, Ed Sullivan, an American television personality, arrived in Tel Aviv. Just like that mythic gunslinger hero, Ed Sullivan would touch the lives of several of those townspeople and change them forever.

Chapter Five

COMING TO AMERICA

For many years "The Ed Sullivan Show" was the most widely-watched television program in America. It ran for twenty-three years, from 1948 until 1971, but its most influential and wildly successful time was during the 1950s. On most Sunday evenings, almost every television set in America was tuned in to this tremendously popular CBS show. It was a variety show. Each program featured a number of different acts, such as singers, dancers, comedians, musicians, circus performers, ventriloquists, and even animals.

The show had a most unlikely host. His name was Ed Sullivan. He was a newspaper columnist who had always wanted desperately to become a star in show business. Unfortunately, Sullivan seemed to have no special talents for such a career. He was a glum-looking Irishman who didn't smile easily and was awkward and ill-at-ease on stage or in front of the cameras. He couldn't sing, dance, or act. His speaking voice was high-pitched and distinctly unpleasant. He was nobody's idea of a performer. Yet Ed Sullivan's dream not only came true, but was surpassed beyond his greatest, most fantastic expectations. He was, in his time, the biggest star on television. His distinctive, awkward, amateurish style and stiff manner were gleefully imitated by mimics and comedians around the world. When anyone said, "We have a *re-e-ely* big *shoo* for you tonight," everyone knew that it was Ed Sullivan's unique style of speech that was being kidded.

Sullivan did, however, have one important talent. It was exactly the one he needed to attract an audience and send ratings soaring. Ed Sullivan was a gifted, intuitive producer. He instinctively seemed to know what people wanted to see. He had the ability to select performers and personalities whom the public would love. This was the gift that made "The Ed Sullivan Show" one of the most popular programs in history and one that had the most influence upon the direction that television broadcasting would subsequently take.

"The Ed Sullivan Show" consistently featured entertainers who would go on to become not only popular with the public, but often show business legends. Some of the already known performers whom he brought even more to the attention of the tube-glued public were: comedian Bob Hope, actor Humphrey Bogart, opera singers Roberta Peters and Maria Callas, and dancers Rudolf Nureyev and Margot Fonteyn. Perhaps his most famous discoveries were Elvis Presley and the Beatles. In February of 1964, on a show that would become a legend in the annals of television history, Ed Sullivan presented four mop-haired kids from England to his variety show audience. "Ladies and gentlemen ...," he announced, "our ... country has never seen anything like these four young men from Liverpool." That is how the Beatles were first introduced to an enthusiastic American public. After that, the Beatles went on, of course, to make entertainment and rock-and-roll history.

Ed Sullivan was always eager to promote the careers of talented young people. In the mid-1950s he came up with an original idea. He wanted to produce a Caravan of Stars that would feature young performers. It would be an opportunity for gifted children to show what they could do. For some of these young people, it could be the break that would set them on a path to eventual success. This was an idea that appealed to the television host whose own dreams of glory had so miraculously come true.

Also, and perhaps more important for the purposes of "The Ed Sullivan Show," he was certain that the television audiences would love it. Ed Sullivan traveled around the world looking for talent for his proposed "Caravan." During that search, he ended up one evening at Churchill Hall in Haifa, Israel. A stocky, cheerful-looking boy on crutches hobbled awkwardly onto the stage. He sat down on a chair that had been prepared for him and set down his crutches on the floor within easy reach. Placing his violin under his chin, the boy lifted his bow and began to play. Every bit of awkwardness vanished, as if by magic.

Ed Sullivan nodded appreciatively. "I've got to have that kid on my show," he told his wife, Sylvia, who was sitting next to him.

The "kid" was Itzhak Perlman. A short time later, the Perlmans received an important and exciting message from America. The young Israeli violinist had become one of the first performers to be invited to appear with "The Ed Sullivan Caravan of Stars."

A journey to the United States of America! Itzhak to perform on national television! This was a towering event in the modest lives of the Perlmans. A tremendous flurry of activity followed. Plans had to made; clothes and suitcases had to be purchased; and travel arrangements had to be finalized. Chaim decided, reluctantly, that it was not possible for him to leave Tel Aviv. The Caravan of Stars involved not only an appearance on television but also a three-month tour around the United States. There was no way that Chaim could afford to be absent from his business for such a length of time. Much as it pained him to miss his son's American television appearance, Chaim still had the responsibility of supporting his family.

Shoshana and Itzhak had to say goodbye to their husband and father. The sadness of their parting was somewhat eased by the excitement and joy of the great adventure on which they were embarking. Together, Shoshana and Itzhak boarded the large, wide-bodied airplane that would carry them to their destiny across the sea.

Twelve-year-old Itzhak must have been eager and nervous with anticipation. In later years, however, when asked about the twenty-three-hour flight to New York that would make such a difference in his life, he would say, "All I can remember is the lousy chicken served on board."

On February 11, 1958, Itzhak Perlman appeared on "The Ed Sullivan Show." The television audience was touched and impressed by the quiet courage of the smiling, self-possessed boy who struggled onto the stage with braces and crutches. But it was his amazing, virtuoso performance that won the hearts of music lovers. He played several showy and difficult pieces — Rimsky-Korsakov's "Flight of the Bumblebee," along with portions of a Mendelssohn violin concerto and "Polonaise Brillante" by a composer named Wieniawski. When Itzhak had finished, the studio rang with applause. Ed Sullivan grinned with satisfaction at the success of his talented protégé. Shoshana Perlman's soul swelled with pride.

The three-month tour that followed proved to be much more difficult and less rewarding than performing on television. Itzhak and the other gifted children in the show were herded about from town to town in a tiring, boring round of rushed performances. They were scheduled to play in luxury hotels, but their dressing room was usually the kitchen. Here, the young people were forced to wait for long hours until it was time for them to perform. Sometimes, they sat around until well after midnight waiting for the call to come. Then they were brought out into ballrooms to show off their skills to exhausted, often disinterested, audiences who had already wined and dined and were ready to go home.

It was a long and tedious three months, but finally, the tour ended. Itzhak and Shoshana returned to Manhattan. There, they made a momentous decision. New York City was a world center for musical education. The Perlmans realized that the opportunities for advanced studies with outstanding teachers were greater here than in Israel. They decided to remain in New York.

Back in Tel Aviv, Chaim began to make plans to close down his business. Meanwhile, Itzhak and his mother settled down in New York, where they went through a period of culture shock and transition. It was a different world for these two displaced Israelis. New York was immense and confusing. The Perlmans' understanding of English was poor. They didn't know how to get around in the sprawling, unfriendly city or even how to obtain the food they required. The Perlmans had always observed Jewish dietary laws, but here, all they could see were non-kosher restaurants and groceries. With limited funds and an even more limited knowledge of their new home, Itzhak and his mother managed to scrape by on sardines and other such cheap, safe foods.

Things improved when Chaim finally joined his family in New York. Chaim was a hard worker and

Famed violinst Isaac Stern recognized and encouraged Itzhak Perlman's talent, and became his mentor and friend.

managed to provide for his family, even when the only job he could get was folding shirts in a Manhattan laundry for fifty dollars a week. But the first years in America were hard for Itzhak. In Tel Aviv, he had, despite his handicap, managed to live a somewhat normal life. He had gone to the neighborhood school with other kids his age and played with them on the street near his apartment. Now, Itzhak missed his old life. He was homesick for the comfortable, familiar scenes of his native land, for his friends, his street, and his school. Everything was different in New York. Life was more solitary. Instead of attending school, Itzhak studied at home with tutors. This was partly because of his handicap and also because his parents wanted him to have enough time for practice and performing. It was apparent to the Perlmans by now that their son's gifts went far beyond the ordinary. A career as a violinist was certainly a strong possibility.

The Perlmans were struggling financially in the new land. The eminent violinist Isaac Stern came to their assistance. He had recognized Itzhak's tremendous potential when he heard him play in Israel. Stern befriended the Perlmans in New York. He tried to ease their financial plight by arranging for the America-Israel Cultural Foundation and other organizations to sponsor the young violinist and provide financial aid. Through them, Itzhak received and accepted offers to play at Jewish fund-raising dinners. It was a way he could help to support his family. Under the sponsorship of the Zionist Organization of America, he toured twenty American and Canadian cities. Audiences were supportive and enthusiastic wherever the gifted young Israeli violinist appeared. But conditions were often far from ideal. Sometimes, Itzhak had to play against the loud conversation of diners and the sound of waiters moving about the room collecting silverware and rattling dishes. Concentrating on the music was difficult under these circumstances. It was a harrowing introduction to the concert scene for the young performer. Itzhak's debut at Carnegie Hall some years later was, he said, "a breeze in comparison."

Despite problems of money and adjustment to a new country, Itzhak maintained his positive attitude.

People who knew him then remember him as a sweet-tempered youngster. He absolutely refused to consider himself in any way handicapped. Isaac Stern describes the boy's "sunniness" of temperament and his lack of self-pity. "There was complete certainty," Stern says, "that he could do anything he put his mind to." To this day, Stern vividly recalls how Itzhak would joyously stand on one crutch and play table tennis with his other hand.

Ordinary crutches can be a problem for a violinist. They can injure the muscles under the arm. Strong arms are essential for playing the violin. Itzhak's friend and sponsor, Isaac Stern, together with Mrs. Stern who had also taken an interest in the young prodigy, took him to an orthopedic specialist. This doctor was a music lover and an amateur violinist. He understood Itzhak's physical needs and designed a special pair of crutches for him.

Itzhak's supporters and sponsors, including Isaac Stern, the America-Israel Cultural Foundation, and the Zionist Organization of American, assisted the young performer in gaining admission to the Juilliard School, one of the most prestigious music schools in the world. Itzhak's outlook was normally positive and optimistic. But he was not in a particularly hopeful mood when he auditioned for this great opportunity. He had not yet adjusted to his new country and his new life. He was far from his native land—tired, confused, and lonely. He felt that he was not at his best musically. Even under these conditions, however, Dorothy DeLay, the prominent teacher for whom he auditioned, was tremendously impressed. "I had never seen such fingers on a thirteen-year-old," she recalled. "The development of skill was so far beyond that of any other child, it was just startling. He had large hands, a fluent bow arm, exceptional coordination, and superb timing. I could not believe my eyes or ears."

Despite his own misgivings, the prodigy was, of course, accepted at Juilliard. It was an expensive educational institution, and money was short for the Perlmans who were struggling to make ends meet. This problem was solved when the school granted their new student a generous scholarship. Scholarship assistance also came, eventually, from other sources, such as the Katherine Tuck Fund in Detroit and from the America-Israel Cultural Foundation. The representatives of these scholarship committees who heard Itzhak play knew that the money was being well-spent.

Itzhak was now well on his way toward a career as a concert violinist. He never had to attend regular public school in the United States. The New York City Board of Education made a special arrangement permitting him to complete his studies and to gain his high school diploma through private tutoring and standard examinations.

Itzhak spent five years in the preparatory division of Juilliard. Here he was instructed by the finest violin teachers. Among them were Ivan Galamian and his assistant, Dorothy DeLay. Perlman described DeLay as "the kind of teacher who doesn't tell you what to do but inspires you to tell her what you want to do."

Ivan Galamian is known worldwide as one of the greatest violin teachers of the late twentieth century. Galamian had been a virtuoso violinist himself, but he was always turned on by teaching. He seemed to have natural leanings in this direction. Teaching was a skill that came to him without effort. Eventually, Galamian gave up his own concert career and applied his energies to developing the skills of talented young violinists. He was an inspired and gifted teacher, though always strict and demanding. "I try to be patient, letting them find their own way," he said. "The teacher must always bear in mind that the highest good should be for him to make the student self-sufficient." Though often overbearing, Galamian never let a student get away with producing less than his best. "You do things very well up to ninety-five percent," he would often comment to a student. "Now, let's do the last five." There was no time for small talk during lessons with Galamian. Every moment was dedicated to intense work.

Ivan Galamian's ultimate goal was to train his students to be the best soloists, concertmasters, and teachers of their time. He was totally dedicated to this mission, teaching every day from eight in the morning until six at night. He constantly monitored his students' careers and work habits, even telephoning them early in the morning to ask, "Why aren't you practicing?"

Galamian's stern and strict demands did not work for all students, but those, such as Itzhak Perlman, who were, like their teacher, endowed with strong personalities, iron wills, and an inner desire to push themselves to their musical limits, flourished under his demanding supervision.

Several of Galamian's students have achieved top international fame as concert violinists. In addition to Itzhak Perlman, Galamian's students include famous soloists Pinchas Zukerman, Miriam Fried, and Kyung-Wha Chung. Under Galamian's instruction, each of these players achieved his own individual style. According to his best-known student, Itzhak Perlman, Galamian had "an approach to technique that works for ninety people out of a hundred." His teacher, Perlman asserts, knew "exactly what he wanted from a pupil and what each was capable of."

Itzhak's other teacher at Juilliard, Dorothy DeLay, was equally influential in his development. Like Galamian, she demanded the best of her students, but her style was different. Galamian was old-world and authoritarian in manner—a sort of "you *will* do what I say" style. DeLay approached teaching in a more democratic manner. She listened to her students with respect and permitted them to participate in decision-making about their individual methods and goals. Her technical demands upon her students were no less than Galamian's, but she brought more warmth and human understanding to the process. What's more, she was interested in helping them as individuals.

DeLay took a special interest in Itzhak, not only as a musician, but in his growth as a whole human being. She was available to help him with personal matters that had nothing to do with music. She gave her time freely to help him with his needs, even teaching him how to drive a hand-controlled car.

Juilliard was a garden of Eden for Itzhak Perlman. He flourished under the rigorous standards these outstanding teachers demanded. The hours that he had to practice daily were not a chore for the boy. They were a labor of love. He learned English and gradually began to feel more comfortable in his new, adopted country. He especially liked the fact that the teachers and musicians with whom he worked accepted his handicap without a fuss. They were more interested in his abilities as a violinist than in his disability or how he managed to get around.

The newly Americanized boy continued to give solo performances. He also concertized with the Youth Symphony of New York and the National Orchestral Association. His appearance on "The Ed Sullivan Show" had been an exciting, earth-shaking experience, but it was the approval of his teachers and other musicians that gave Itzhak true pleasure. What he desired above all was to be the best violinist he was capable of being, and they were the ones who really knew him—the ones who could help him achieve his goals.

In 1963, five years after Itzhak's arrival in America, when he was seventeen years old, his teachers decided that he was ready to make his debut at Carnegie Hall.

Chapter Six

A CARNEGIE HALL DEBUT

There is an old New York joke that city dwellers like to tell. It is so old that it has many variations. Basically, it goes something like this:

Tourist to cab driver: "How do you get to Carnegie Hall?"

Cab driver (smirking): "Practice!"

At seventeen, Itzhak Perlman had practiced ... and practiced ... and practiced. Since the age of five, the violin had been his most constant and trusted companion. Nothing, not even the pain and unceasing complications of polio and paralysis could make him give up his musical dreams. Day after day, month after month, year after year, he had practiced and studied many hours each day. He had shown a natural affinity for the violin from the beginning, but talent alone is never enough, especially with an instrument as complex and difficult to master as the violin. Even the most gifted musician must put in long, grueling hours of study and effort if he or she is to achieve full potential as an artist. Itzhak had done this despite a handicap that could easily have overpowered all ambitions. He would keep on doing it. But in 1963, his teachers felt that he was ready for that milestone in the life of any concert musician—a Carnegie Hall debut.

Located in Manhattan, Carnegie Hall is the leading concert hall in America, and one of the most prestigious in the world. It is so famous that a letter addressed simply, "Carnegie Hall, U.S.A." will be delivered correctly by the post office. In its recital halls, rooms, and auditoriums have appeared not only great orchestras and classical musicians, but popular singers and groups, including jazz, country, and rock-and-roll musicians. Louis Armstrong, Duke Ellington, and Benny Goodman all performed at Carnegie Hall. So did Judy Garland, Peter Allen, Arlo Guthrie, and the Rolling Stones. Fiery lecturers, impassioned debaters, flamboyant opera singers, actors, and even world-renowned statesmen and politicians have faced audiences in the famous building. U.S. Presidents Woodrow Wilson and Theodore Roosevelt spoke there as did British World War II prime minister and famed orator, Winston Churchill.

It is for aspiring classical musicians, however, that Carnegie is a name that evokes magic and longing. It is their mecca, their gate to paradise. It can also be the beginning of a descent into failure and oblivion. A Carnegie Hall debut is simultaneously desired and feared. It is a test that some pass and some do not. A glorious career can have its start here. Just as frequently, a promising beginning can be stifled and ended there.

What is this building that can evoke such strong emotion among performers? Basically, it is a music hall. In fact, that was its name when it was built in the last decade of the nineteenth century with the help of an endowment from multi-millionaire industrialist Andrew Carnegie. Architect William Burnet Tuthill designed the structure in a grand style. It was envisioned as a home for the cultural life of the city and a source of pride to the nation.

The gala opening performance at the Music Hall took place with much fanfare on May 5, 1891. Society's elite, wearing their most fashionable clothes and jewels, filled the auditorium to overflowing. An internationally-famed cast was featured in the program. It included visiting Russian composer Peter Ilyitch Tchaikovsky, who had written such well-known works as *The Nutcracker* and *Sleeping Beauty*. One newspaper columnist who was covering the event reported breathlessly, "Tonight, the most beautiful Music Hall in the world was consecrated to the loveliest of the arts."

There is something about this Music Hall that is even more important to the musicians who perform there and to the audiences who come to hear them than the building's hallowed history. Carnegie Hall boasts one of the best sound systems of any concert auditorium in the world. Its acoustics have been called "a marvel," "incredible," and "absolutely perfect."

No one seems to know exactly why the acoustics at Carnegie are so outstanding. At one time it was believed that the marvelous sound was due to the presence of a solid rock bed underneath the building. This particular myth was squashed when it was discovered that, contrary to the popular legend, Carnegie Hall is built over a bubbling spring-fed pond. Credit for the perfection of sound is sometimes given to the skilled masonry that was involved in the construction. Others swear that it is the extensive use of seasoned wood that induces this effect. Every "expert" has his or her own explanation for Carnegie's perfection of sound.

Whatever the reason—and none of the explanations are more than educated guesses — the acoustics at Carnegie Hall have inspired musical artists through the years to produce their best work. It is said that every note played can be heard accurately from every seat in the auditorium. Each instrument and each voice can find its ultimate purity of sound within these walls. The dark side to this is that tones that are less than perfect are amplified and exaggerated. There is no way for a performer to hide his mistakes. In Carnegie Hall these lapses stand out like huge warts upon one's face. They cannot be disguised.

Every young performer who contemplates a career as a concert musician must endure the rigors of a Carnegie Hall debut. This significant event usually consists of the young artist, his manager, family, and friends gathering together in Recital Hall, one of the smaller auditoriums in the building. Sometimes, one of the larger rooms is needed, especially if the performer has built up a following as a result of solo performances before this debut. Also present are several reviewers or music critics who will write a brief review of the event to be published in the next day's newspapers. It is this scrutiny by professional critics that is usually the most dreaded aspect of a Carnegie Hall debut. A mediocre review can be crushing to the young musician's tender ego. A bad one can ruin his career before it really begins.

It was under such circumstances, on Tuesday evening, March 5, 1963, at 8 p.m., that Itzhak Perlman hobbled, with the aid of his crutches, onto the stage of Carnegie Hall. The time had come for his debut performance at the great testing ground of classical music. Itzhak did not appear alone in a small recital hall as some young performers do when making their Carnegie debuts. Having already begun to make a name for himself as a soloist, Perlman performed as part of a National Orchestral Association concert conducted by well-known maestro John Bennett. He played a fairly difficult piece, Wieniawski's Violin Concerto No. 1 in F Sharp Minor.

Despite his many previous solo performances and the hours of intense practice he had given to this piece, Itzhak was somewhat nervous at first. This was, after all, his first appearance within these venerated walls. The Carnegie mystique hung heavy upon the shoulders of the young violinist. But once the concert began and he was able to concentrate his heart and mind upon the music itself, all Itzhak's dedicated preparation paid off and he was able to perform flawlessly.

When the concert had ended, however, and the applause had died down, the true agony of uncertainty began — waiting for the judgment of the critics. What would they say? Itzhak believed he had played well. This had been confirmed by those who were present. But who ever could tell what a critic might decide?

The reviews were not scheduled to appear in the newspapers until the following day. First, a long, long night of suspense had to be endured. As it turned out, all the nervous uncertainty and expectation were for nothing. The reviews of Itzhak Perlman's Carnegie Hall debut would not appear in the daily newspapers. In fact, nothing would be reported that day because there was a newspaper strike in New York, and the papers were not published.

This was a great disappointment to the young violinist. Although he feared the critics' disdain, he was eager for their approval. He wanted his work to be noticed, to be applauded. Now, it seemed as though this great moment of his life as a musician would pass unheeded and without public comment.

It was bad luck that the newspaper strike occurred on the day following Itzhak's performance. His Carnegie Hall debut went unreported by the press thanks to the unforeseen circumstance of the newspaper strike. But Itzhak's first appearance at the famed hall did not, as he feared, go by completely unnoticed. Those who had attended the concert were tremendously impressed by his extraordinary ability, and the gifted young violinist was brought to the attention of masters in the field such as Isaac Stern and Yehudi Menuhin, themselves leading violinists of the day.

Isaac Stern had heard Perlman play years earlier, when Itzhak was still a child in Israel. He had offered the Perlmans emotional support during their first difficult years in America and had helped them obtain financial help as well. Stern was impressed by the great strides the young performer had made. His earlier predictions that a rare talent had come upon the musical scene were confirmed. Watching and listening to the seventeen-year-old performer, Stern could see that Itzhak had the potential to be a truly great violinist. "The violin is as natural to him to play," Stern remarked, "as it is for you and me to breathe."

Isaac Stern is not only a great artist, but also a generous, selfless human being. Envy of another person's musical abilities is foreign to his nature. Instead, he has always gone out of his way to befriend and nurture young musicians. He immediately recognized and appreciated Itzhak Perlman's gifts. From the beginning, the older artist was a true friend and guide to Itzhak Perlman. Stern was, as he puts it himself, "a kind of good, older brother who listened to him and guided him and, if necessary, read him the rules of the game for himself." Isaac Stern brought Itzhak Perlman into contact with Sol Hurok, a noted impresario and concert producer, who began to arrange performances for the young prodigy.

Isaac Stern also served as one of the judges in an important musical competition sponsored by an organization called the Leventritt Foundation. This was one of the most prestigious and demanding competitions in the world of music, officially called the International

Edgar M. Leventritt Contest and was founded in 1940 in memory of Edgar M. Leventritt, a New York lawyer.

Edgar M. Leventritt was a dedicated lover of classical music. He was also an excellent amateur musician in his own right. After his death, his daughter established the Edgar M. Leventritt Foundation in his memory. She explained, "My father was crazy about young artists and at the time he died, the idea of an international competition for orchestral prizes was new. Our purpose was to launch young artists, to set a standard for teachers and performers, and to make it truly international."

The contest that Edgar Leventritt inspired eventually grew to be one of the most important annual events in the music world. In alternate years, the Leventritt competition was open to pianists. In the other years, it was held for violinists. Six months before the date of the contest, notices were sent to music schools, teachers, and various musical organizations.

Aspiring artists from around the world sent in applications for this honor. They applied even though they knew that, if chosen to participate, they would be letting themselves in for a grueling ordeal. They would be coming up against the very best young musicians in the world, and only one of them could win. The competition was fierce and the judges were incisive and demanding. Most contestants who entered the competition would agree with one young performer who, when the competition was over, complained wearily, "I've never had to go through pressure like this. In a concert, if you miss a note, you don't worry. Here, you immediately feel it's a point against you." Most of these contestants didn't have the additional problems of a physical handicap. Even so, the stress they were under could be overwhelming. Outsiders sometimes wondered why they did it. Evidently it was because, in their hearts, each one believed that he or she could win.

Itzhak Perlman's teachers and friends persuaded him to enter the Leventritt Competition that was held in April 1964. The winner that year would receive a one thousand dollar cash prize. Even more important,

Itzhak Perlman, age seventeen, at the time of the Leventritt Competition. (Photo courtesy of NYT Pictures.)

the lucky victor would be guaranteed nationwide publicity as well as career-building solo appearances with the major symphony orchestras of New York, Cleveland, Detroit, Pittsburgh, Buffalo, Denver, and New Haven.

There were forty applicants when the Leventritt Competition began that year. Itzhak was the youngest of ten semi-finalists. Six additional talented performers were eliminated in these grueling semi-finals. On April 21st, 1964, four finalists, including Itzhak Perlman, performed at Carnegie Hall before a distinguished and demanding group of thirteen judges. This panel included violinist Isaac Stern, who had been Itzhak's champion and mentor since his arrival in the United States, conductors George Szell and Lukas Foss, and other music notables.

In addition to Itzhak Perlman, the finalists included David Abel from California, Charles Castleman of Boston, and Takako Nishizaki from Japan. Each finalist played for about thirty-five minutes in front of the panel of judges. There was also an audience of about four hundred spectators, including members of the press. It was a gruelling challenge for any young musician, but the finalists were serious, dedicated violinists and well-prepared. They were all superb, but three of them were destined to be deeply disappointed. When the results were in, it turned out that Itzhak Perlman, struggling onstage with his crutches, the only one who had had to play seated, came out in first place, winning the coveted prize. He played selections from Tchaikovsky, Mozart, Bach, and Wieniawski, and despite the stress and strain of competition, he had never played better.

This time, Itzhak was not denied his reviews and acclamations in the press. The critics raved about his technique and his outstanding musical gifts. To

Itzhak's relief, they did not make a big deal out of his disability, but concentrated instead upon his performance as an artist. He had hated some of the articles that had been printed about him when he first came to the United States to perform. "Handicapped violinist pretty good despite disability," or "As he went on the stage hobbling on his shining aluminum crutches and very heavily sat down ... but afterwards, we forgot all about it and it was just music." Itzhak detested the coupling of his disability with his skill as an artist. He wanted to be judged solely on the basis of his abilities as a violinist, just like anyone else.

The critics who reviewed the Leventritt finals for the most part ignored his handicap or mentioned it only in passing. They described instead the excellence of Itzhak Perlman's playing. Music critic William Bender in the *New York Herald Tribune* cited his "big, rich tone" and "faultless intonation." "Most important of all," Bender enthused, "was the warmth and individuality he brought to the first movement of the Tchaikovsky Violin Concerto .... He clearly outdistanced his worthy rivals, and by a wide margin." It was obvious to the seasoned critic that this young man had something special that raised him above even the best of his contemporaries.

Somehow, however, unusual circumstances appeared to be attracted to Itzhak Perlman like moths to a flame. He could not seem to avoid being singled out for special attention by events and complications that had nothing whatsoever to do with his abilities as a concert violinist. At the Leventritt Contest, it was not the young winner's physical handicap that captured the reporters' sharp noses for news, but another intriguing incident that set the typewriter keys of the journalists clicking and clacking with excitement.

Perlman himself did not yet own a truly fine violin.

His teachers at Juilliard didn't want him to be at a disadvantage in the competition by having to use a second-rate instrument. They arranged for him to borrow a priceless, two hundred-year-old Guarnerius violin from Juilliard's rare instrument collection to use for the Leventritt finals. It was a marvelously sensitive instrument, valued anywhere from $25,000 to $40,000, or even more, and Perlman performed flawlessly upon it.

When Itzhak finished his performance and left the stage, he went to a large area called the "Orchestra Room" to await the verdict. His mother, Shoshana Perlman, accompanied him. They carefully placed the precious Guarnerius on a chair and covered it with Mrs. Perlman's coat. When the decision of the judges was about to be announced, Itzhak went out into the hall where he could hear better, leaving his mother to guard the violin.

Immediately after the verdict announcing his triumph, Itzhak was swept up in a pandemonium of celebration. Friends and well-wishers rushed backstage to congratulate him. Soon, Itzhak was surrounded by a happy, excited crowd. Mrs. Perlman, ecstatic with joy at her son's great success, joined them.

The Guarnerius was still in the Orchestra Room, under Mrs. Perlman's coat. It was left unguarded for only a few minutes. But when Itzhak and his mother returned to the Orchestra Room to retrieve the violin, to their horror they discovered that it was gone. The rare and irreplaceable violin had disappeared. It had been stolen!

This was newsworthy indeed! It was the sort of rare, bizarre twist that the media thrives upon. The reviewers reported this strange and intriguing occurrence in such detail that it completely overshadowed the true meaning of the Leventritt competition and

Itzhak's triumph there. "*Violinist Wins Prize, Loses a Guarnerius,*" smirked the banner headline in the *New York Times*. Despite the warm and appreciative review the critic gave to Perlman's artistry, it was this striking, outlandish headline that attracted attention and stayed in people's minds.

The missing violin was discovered the next day in a small pawnshop in Times Square. Whoever had stolen the instrument evidently had no idea of its true value. Nor did the pawnbroker. The irreplaceable Guarnerius had been pawned for a mere fifteen dollars. As Perlman himself wryly noted, "The thief obviously was not a musician."

A few weeks after the Leventritt, Itzhak Perlman again borrowed the now-famous Guarnerius from Juilliard. This time he used it for a concert in Washington, D.C. with the National Symphony Orchestra. Irving Lowens, music critic for the *Washington Evening Star* attended the performance. In his column the following day, Lowens reported that the much publicized instrument's "characteristically rich, burnished tone ... was used to wonderful advantage" and that Perlman received an enthusiastic standing ovation "on the basis of his talent alone."

Paul Hume reviewed the same concert in the *Washington Post*. In his column, Hume announced that "courage comes in many forms. Last night, National Symphony Orchestra subscribers had an unusual opportunity to salute courage coupled with a superior display of musical art." Hume wrote admiringly about how the eighteen-year-old violinist used crutches to get onstage. "This takes a kind of guts," the critic noted, "that those who have not been faced with a similar challenge cannot begin to comprehend." After describing Itzhak's "sensuous tone" and "supple phrasing," Hume predicted that here was one young classical performer who was definitely "headed for a large career."

These words were sweet to Itzhak. For it was, after all, his abilities as a violinist that meant the most to him. Whatever the reason, however, musical or otherwise, the Leventritt Competition had catapulted eighteen-year-old Itzhak Perlman into a prominence and a public image rare for a classical performer. In the years that followed, that stardom grew steadily alongside Perlman's own development as a human being and as a mature musician.

Chapter Seven

SUCCESS IN CAREER AND ROMANCE

Many young classical soloists enter a variety of competitions in order to boost their careers. Itzhak Perlman decided that the Leventritt would be the last contest for him. "I won it—I quit," he said, in his usual down-to-earth, tell-it-like-it-is style. He believed that the problems and pressures involved in competing with other violinists, who were equally as good as oneself, definitely outweighed any possible benefits.

Besides, so far as Itzhak's career was concerned, it really didn't seem to be necessary to enter competitions in order to get opportunities to perform and to develop as a musician. After the Leventritt, under the guidance of famed impresario Sol Hurok, who was now his agent, Itzhak entered upon a coast-to-coast tour of thirty American cities. In addition, he returned, in triumph, to appear once again on television on "The Ed Sullivan Show," where he had begun his career in the United States.

In October 1964, the same year he won the Leventritt Competition, Itzhak performed Tchaikovsky's Violin Concerto with the National Symphony Orchestra in Washington, and again at Carnegie Hall with the Israel National Youth Symphony Orchestra. In this, as in other performances, critics responded to the inspired playing of the young violinist with the delight with which one discovers a new and brilliant star in the heavens. They wrote that he "stole the show." William Bender, music critic for the *New York Herald Tribune* noted that the nineteen-year-old violinist brought to his playing "a lyricism and youthful exuberance that made the old favorite sound as though it had been written the day before." He called Itzhak "one of the finest violinists of his generation," and predicted "a distinguished career" for him. "His flow of pure, sweet tone is unceasing," Bender enthused. "His bow arm is ... strong and steady, and the fingering ... is dazzling swift and accurate. There is a joy and bounce to his playing that had old-timers reaching back in their memories to the days of a youthful Heifetz."

The resemblance to Jascha Heifetz was echoed by *Chicago Daily News* critic Donal J. Henahan after a concert in that city the following year. "Those of us who were not listening to violin recitals half a century ago sometimes wonder what it must have been like to hear the teenage Heifetz for the first time. Some idea of that temperature-raising experience probably was conveyed this weekend by the twenty-year-old Itzhak Perlman's recital .... It will be recalled as a major musical event by all lucky enough to have heard it." Henahan added this "tongue-in-cheek" comment: "It was possible to imagine that Itzhak Perlman was born with a violin protruding from his left clavicle and never had to learn to play it anymore than he had to learn to breathe."

The ghost of Heifetz was also invoked by Louis Biancolli in the *New York World Telegram* on October 29, 1965. After describing the performer's "staggering display of technique in Sibelius' Violin Concerto," the critic added, "To be so handicapped, to be only twenty and to perform the work as perhaps only Heifetz performed it is to bring back the age of miracles."

For Itzhak, the miracle must surely have been the coupling of his name with that of the incomparable master. To be so glowingly compared to the idol of his childhood—Jascha Heifetz—that was sweet praise indeed to Itzhak.

Other reviews of the young violinist's appearances were equally flattering. But Itzhak's studies at Juilliard continued. So did his constant practicing and striving for improvement. His performances were brilliant, but he was still young, still developing as a musical interpreter and as a master of his instrument.

In addition to lessons at Juilliard, Itzhak spent his summers studying at the Meadowmount colony. This was a school for string players located amid the beautiful, serene surroundings of the Adirondack Mountains in New York state. Meadowmount was run by Ivan Galamian, and so it was natural that Galamian's most gifted pupil should come there each summer to study. Itzhak spent eight happy summers at Meadowmount. "I loved every minute," he recalled. "The atmosphere was such that you were totally moved into achieving. Everybody around you was practicing and showing off." Another former Meadowmount camper recalls it somewhat differently, as "slave labor ... you had to get up and practice all day long." But even this student admits that though everyone complained and swore never to return, "somewhere, we all loved it."

In the summer of 1963, the year previous to his victory at the Leventritt, seventeen-year-old Itzhak Perlman managed to do more at Meadowmount than just practice the violin and concertize. That summer, love burst into the life of the youthful virtuoso. It came in the form of an attractive young woman named Toby Friedlander.

Toby Friedlander was a promising violin student

at the colony that summer of 1963. She was twenty, three years older than Itzhak, and a graduate student at Juilliard. At one student performance that year, she watched with interest and sympathy as a curly-haired, handsome, but crippled young performer hobbled onto the stage. He sat down, grinned cheerfully, raised his bow, and began to play. Any pity Toby might have been feeling for the disabled violinist disappeared almost immediately. She listened with incredulous awe to his rendition of "Tzigane" by Maurice Ravel, an appropriately romantic composition. Never had she heard it played with such skill, spirit, and sensitivity.

Toby's heart was pierced, both as a musician and as a woman. She had to meet this violinist who could work such magic. She just had to! After the performance, Toby rushed backstage to congratulate the unassuming boy who had just given her the most heartfelt musical experience of her life. She felt as if she had become possessed by the music he had created. Toby also found his appearance intensely attractive. She felt an overwhelming desire to stay near him forever. She was an impulsive young woman. In her excitement and enthusiastic confusion, she even asked him to marry her right then and there.

Poor Itzhak! He didn't know what to make of this wild-looking young woman who had descended on him with such passionate fervor. He was completely inexperienced with girls. His life until then had been single-mindedly devoted to one purpose and one goal only—mastering the violin. He had never had the time nor the opportunity to meet girls. As a matter of fact, he had never even been out on a date.

Itzhak stared at the girl speechless. He was certain that she must be at least somewhat deranged. Later, however, when Toby finally calmed down, Itzhak realized that her extreme behavior had only been an impulsive reaction to his performance of the "Tzigane." The whole encounter suddenly began to seem quite romantic, especially when Itzhak became aware that in addition to having an intense love of music, the girl was very pretty indeed. It was not difficult at all for him to become friends with Toby Friedlander.

For Toby, it had been love at first sight (and sound). She did everything she could to promote a friendship with the fellow student who had stolen her heart with his music. Itzhak had never been shy. He was, in fact, quite outgoing and talkative. But he had never given any thought or energy to a relationship with a girl. It was not a priority for him at this time in his life.

Toby soon recognized Itzhak's inexperience and lack of interest. She later admitted that she plotted and maneuvered to further their relationship. "I had to develop a friendship," she said, "because I knew he wasn't ready for marriage yet."

Toby was ready, however, and she knew exactly who it was she wanted to marry. She realized that the time was not right for Itzhak and so she was patient. She befriended and charmed him at Meadowmount. Back in New York, she discovered to her delight that she and Itzhak both lived in the same upper west side neighborhood of Manhattan. Boldly, she telephoned him and brought classical records to his apartment for them to listen to together. Their friendship grew steadily closer, but it was slow going and frustrating to Toby. She bided her time. A year, two years, three years went by with Itzhak never showing any desire to be more than a good friend. Toby pressed on, ever hopeful.

Meanwhile, Itzhak's career as a concert violinist was blossoming. Under impresario Sol Hurok's guidance, he began to appear more and more frequently with leading orchestras. The critics were enthusiastic and encouraging. The public was learning to love him, not only for his musical talent but also for his charming, outgoing, often funny and endearing personality.

In January 1965 Itzhak returned to his native land, Israel. It was the first time he had been back since departing with his mother on that fateful airplane trip that had carried him across the seas to musical adventures in America. That had been seven years earlier. When he left, he had been just a crippled boy of twelve, with talent. Now, he was on the verge of becoming one of the most acclaimed violinists of his generation.

Itzhak gave a series of eight concerts in Israel, crisscrossing the tiny country and appearing at all the major concert halls. It was a triumphant return. He was received with an outpouring of love, pride, and appreciation. The music critic for the Israeli newspaper *Haaretz* wrote, "Last week, an extraordinary talent came to Israel. His ability and general knowledge of music are so superb ... that his technique and manual ability are taken as a matter of course ... Perlman creates a tonal feeling which sings in the ear and shakes the soul."

At Tel Aviv's Mann Auditorium, in the city of Itzhak's birth, the audience stood up and applauded wildly for a full fifteen minutes after he performed concertos by Tchaikovsky and Sibelius with the Israel Philharmonic Orchestra. They shouted for an encore. This is something that is rarely done by Israeli audiences. Itzhak had pierced the hearts of his countrymen and women with his music. This was one of the most emotional experiences of his life. "Every kid in Israel dreams that one day he's going to play with the IPO," he said wistfully, "and then the dream comes true." It was a moment that the young violinist would remember forever.

In May of the same year, Itzhak performed with the

New York Philharmonic Orchestra. The audience called him back to the stage five times with loud, incessant applause. They couldn't get enough of him. Itzhak was a few months short of twenty years of age. He had proven himself to be an artist of the first caliber. A *New York Times* reviewer wrote about a subsequent concert, "Truly a sensational violinist ... listening to him play produced joy on every level—technical, musical, and above all the human. For the burly young man has that extra quality that raises music above technicalities, and that is heart."

The performances and rave reviews continued. Meanwhile, in New York, Toby Friedlander was beginning to wonder whether her quest to become more than a friend to Itzhak was hopeless, perhaps even a complete waste of time. Three years had passed since their first meeting at Meadowmount. Itzhak was a delightful friend. He was charming, humorous, and always fun to be with, and they shared the same passionate devotion to music and to the violin. But Toby began to despair of ever becoming anything more than a good friend to Itzhak. Too many years were going by without any sign of commitment. Finally, Toby made up her mind to give up.

"I decided no man was worth it and washed my hands of him," she said.

Itzhak couldn't help but notice that his once devoted friend had cooled off. He realized that he missed her. In fact, it seemed, to his surprise, that he missed her very much indeed. He wanted her companionship and her devotion. Slowly, Itzhak began to become aware of his own true feelings. He realized, with a shock, that he was in love with Toby Friedlander.

Toby! Suddenly, Itzhak found it hard to concentrate on anything else. The tables had turned. Toby had drifted away, and now Itzhak had become the pursuer.

Itzhak remembered their first meeting at Meadowmount, when Toby had impulsively asked him to marry her. He had been too young then. He hadn't been ready. But he was ready now, and he wanted Toby to marry him.

But now, after all this time, Toby wasn't sure. She had tried so hard and so long. Perhaps they weren't right for each other after all. It took a year and a half of intense, persistent courting for Itzhak to convince her that they were indeed meant for one another.

On Thursday, January 5, 1967, Itzhak's representatives issued a press release headed, "ITZHAK PERLMAN, ISRAELI VIOLINIST, TO MARRY MISS FRIEDLANDER THIS EVENING."

Further details were given. "Miss Toby Lynn Friedlander, daughter of Mr. and Mrs. Harold Friedlander ... will be married this evening to the Israeli violinist, Itzhak Perlman, son of Mr. and Mrs. Chaim Perlman ... The ceremony will be performed by Rabbi Avraham Soltis ... at the America-Israel-Culture House ... Miss Friedlander, a violinist studying at the Juilliard School of Music, is a graduate of the High School of Music and Art. The bridegroom, winner of the 1964 Leventritt Award and prominent soloist with ... major orchestras, has been a resident of New York since he first arrived here to study in 1958, when he was thirteen."

The announcement went on to name the bridal attendants and best man and to note that a number of persons prominent in the musical world would be among the guests.

Toby Friedlander had finally become Toby Perlman.

Itzhak and Toby Perlman continued to live on Manhattan's upper west side where they had both spent their teenage years. Eventually, they moved into a spacious, eleven-room co-op overlooking the Hudson

River. The apartment had once belonged to legendary baseball great Babe Ruth. Not long afterwards, the first of their five children was born. Itzhak Perlman was now not only a violinist whose star was on the ascendancy, but also a family man. The latter role was becoming infinitely more important to him.

Chapter Eight

EXPANDING HIS MUSICAL HORIZONS

Still in his early twenties, Itzhak Perlman had already won worldwide fame as a violinist. He soon became one of the most sought-after performers on Sol Hurok's list of artists and was solidly booked year-round to perform at concert halls in the United States and abroad. Audiences and critics continued to be stunned by his talent.

"There is nothing in the whole field of violin playing that he cannot do with his left hand," wrote one critic. "I cannot remember when a first encounter with a violinist has made such an impression."

After a 1966 concert in Beverly Hills, *Los Angeles Times* reviewer Albert Goldberg exclaimed, "Just when the race of really great violinists was threatening to become extinct ... along comes young Itzhak Perlman to rescue the torch and ... renew the waning popularity of the instrument .... He is the major talent among the younger generation of fiddlers and the missing link in the great tradition."

Itzhak's first appearance with the New York Philharmonic in 1965 brought the audience to its feet. They rewarded the soloist with five curtain calls. "At age twenty, he is already an artist of the first rank," wrote the *New York Times*. The *Herald Tribune* critic was equally enthusiastic, acclaiming the young violinist's "astonishing command of his instrument and the smooth melting sound that he draws from it," and adding, "Mr. Perlman showed ... not only what a great violinist he is going to be, but how thoroughly equipped he already is."

It would be easy for a young performer to let such acclaim go to his head. But Itzhak didn't have the time to sit back and bask in the sunshine of critical applause. He was too busy studying and practicing. The violin is a stern taskmaster. Intensive daily practice is necessary to keep up one's skills and techniques. Furthermore, as a musical artist, there is no end to the ongoing learning that must take place. There is always more to be mastered—better techniques, new pieces to learn, a deeper understanding of the music that is already known. Mastering a musical instrument, especially one as complex and capable of varied nuances as the violin, is not the same as becoming a skilled typist. Once you have memorized the typewriter keyboard, you can always strive to type faster and more accurately, but that is the complete extent to which you can aspire. Music leads one into an endless maze of possibilities and interpretations. A musician can perform one phrase the same way for years, and then, quite suddenly, see a new and truer way of interpreting the same combination of notes. For an artist, the process of growing and expanding goes on forever.

For Itzhak Perlman, there were additional dimensions of music and life to explore besides the repertoire of the classical violin. He did not scorn other kinds of musical expression or other ways of performing. As a result, the name Itzhak Perlman began to be recognized even by mainstream audiences. Eventually, the cheerful, curly-haired violinist with a cherubic grin and ready wit became better known than almost any other classical soloist in the world. Most serious classical performers are familiar only to that small segment of the public that takes a strong interest in classical music. Itzhak Perlman's name gradually came to be known by ordinary people, many of whom do not usually pay much attention to classical music. This unprecedented name-recognition was due, in large measure, to the extensive exposure he was given on television.

Itzhak Perlman turned out to be the violin virtuoso for the television age. After all, his first appearance in America had been on television, on Ed Sullivan's show, when Itzhak was only twelve and a half. From the beginning, he felt at home in that medium and continued to make extensive use of it. As the years went by, he gave many concert performances on television. In addition, he appeared on such diverse programs as "60 Minutes," "The Tonight Show," "Sesame Street," and various commercials. Once, Itzhak was even a guest on "The Frugal Gourmet" program on public television, where he was so eager to demonstrate to the world his culinary skills and repertoire of jokes about food that he practically took over the show and hardly let the host get a word in edgewise.

Many traditionalists have judged Perlman harshly in this light. They accused him of catering to the mass media. He received special criticism for participating in commercials. Itzhak countered by pointing out that "the commercials that I've chosen to make do not represent something I would feel uncomfortable with. The fact that people will ask you to make a commercial is an indication that you have a kind of public persona." He went on to say, "My start in the United States was on television, and so television is something I feel comfortable with."

One might think that Itzhak Perlman, of all people,

would not have been at ease with such a visual medium because of his disability. Exactly the opposite seems to be the case. This is probably because Itzhak Perlman has other attributes that make him the perfect television performer. Foremost among these is his outgoing, expansive personality. He seems to feel at home with all sorts of people and in all sorts of situations. He is extroverted, talkative, and, most of all, loves to clown around. His friendly, outgoing manner grew even more self-assured along with his success.

Itzhak discovered that he liked to talk, not only about music, composers, the violin, and his career, but about the many other subjects in which he had developed an interest. Soon after his arrival in New York, Itzhak had become a diehard Yankees fan. Later, he could be as enthusiastic discussing baseball with the star pitcher of the Kansas City Royals as he was talking about the differences between performing with a symphony orchestra or with a chamber music group. He grew fond of basketball, too. He and Toby often managed to attend games of the New York Knicks.

And he usually managed to throw in a joke or two, accompanied by what music critic Donal Henahan described as a "great, booming, bass-baritone laugh." When Itzhak was asked by Mike Wallace on a "60 Minutes" interview why it was that so many important violinists are Jewish, Itzhak replied (with tongue in cheek), "You see, our fingers are circumcised ... which gives it a very good dexterity, you know, particularly in the pinky."

Early on, Itzhak developed a passion for food. As a result, he has always been particularly fond of food jokes, especially terrible ones, such as: "Two peanuts were walking in Central Park; one was assaulted," or "I'm going on a seafood diet next week. I see the food and eat it."

A special opportunity to give full expression to his love of clowning came during the several appearances Itzhak has made on "Sesame Street," the children's educational television program, where he was a great hit with cast and audience alike. In one episode, taped in 1980, Itzhak played the violin for Oscar the Grouch, who had just popped out of a crumpled garbage can. Itzhak takes great pleasure in such seemingly oddball appearances. He thinks that it is important for children to be confronted with disabilities and to realize that they are a part of life. Besides, he truly enjoyed the experience of being on "Sesame Street." Somehow managing to keep a straight face, he solemnly declared that "one of my goals in life was to make music with Oscar the Grouch."

During the years that followed, Itzhak Perlman made other appearances, too, that were not consistent with the stereotype of a "serious" classical musician. He once sang with superstar opera singer Luciano Pavarotti in a performance of the opera *Tosca* at Lincoln Center. Of that experience he commented, "The first thing that came to my mind is that I'm going to take the job of a poor bass baritone who could sing the jailer." Itzhak feared that he would be taking away some singer's livelihood. When assured that the part would be cut from the performance if he didn't do it, Perlman finally agreed. But "I agonized," he recalled. "I have never practiced so hard in my life."

Itzhak was never a snob when it came to music. Through the years he learned to appreciate and enjoy other sorts of music besides that usually associated with classical violin performers. He has appeared on television with pop singers like John Denver and recorded country music and rag. Once at an outdoor cookout in Aspen, Colorado, Itzhak playfully seized a fiddle from one of the members of the little band that

Itzhak Perlman appeared on Sesame Street *with Oscar the Grouch. (Photo courtesy of Children's Television Workshop, © 1991.)*

was entertaining the party-goers and treated the guests to a dazzling version of "Turkey in the Straw."

Always ready to expand his musical horizons, Itzhak also developed a great interest in jazz. He performed energetically with several jazz combos. Composer/conductor Andre Previn wrote a jazz album expressly for Itzhak, which he recorded with jazz artists Red Mitchell on bass, Shelly Mann on drums, Jim Hall on guitar, and Andre Previn at the piano. It was issued under the title, "A Different Kind of Blues."

Itzhak was not even reluctant to demonstrate his fondness for jazz and popular music within the hallowed corridors of Carnegie Hall. On January 5, 1976, he performed there with his own version of Scott Joplin's "Pineapple Rag," as well as some astounding variations on that old standby "Yankee Doodle."

In addition to concerts and television appearances,

Itzhak also began to record extensively. He made records of almost all classical works in the violin repertoire for Angel, London, RCA, and Deutsche Gramophone labels.

Itzhak's television appearances through the years made him well-known to audiences and helped to gain for him the type of adoration that is usually reserved for rock stars. Some serious musicians and critics continued to look upon such carryings-on with disapproval. Itzhak believed, however, that his appearances on popular media were promoting the cause of classical music. "In a sense," he remarked, "it's the strongest way to bring more music to more people. My being on talk shows has familiarized countless people with fiddle playing. A lot of people come to my concerts who've never been to a concert before." When some music critics complained that such pop appearances only blurred differences between musical styles, Itzhak countered, "Let me tell you something about music critics. I feel that a music critic has a very tough job ... a music critic in a city like New York goes to many concerts a week and after a while, he sits there and says, 'So come on, excite me.' It's like a Catch-22," Itzhak complained. "To be outrageous makes for better reading. You don't hear about the nice critics, you hear about the mean ones who criticized Tchaikovsky's Violin Concerto (at its premiere) and said the violin was beaten black and blue."

Actually, however, Itzhak Perlman has little cause to complain about music critics. It was not only audiences who were touched and moved by the beauty of the music he created for them, but the critics as well. The glowing reviews that they wrote were stepping-stones in his career. This was as true in the early years of that career as it proved to be when he grew in stature as a performer. While still in his teens, he was already getting standing ovations from the audience. This ecstatic response was echoed by music reviewers with words such as, "His tone at all times was one of supreme beauty"; "Close your eyes and you could easily imagine that Isaac Stern was playing the lovely andante"; "The standing ovation ... was merited on the basis of his talent alone"; "An astonishingly accomplished soloist ... despite his tender years"; or "Courage coupled with a superior display of musical art."

As Itzhak grew in years, his musical gifts only deepened, and this was noted by the critics. Donal Henahan, writing in the *New York Times*, described a Carnegie Hall performance in 1975 as "one of those affairs at which complete strangers smile at one another and shake their heads in happy mutual wonder." The reviewer also took note of Itzhak's growing skill. "Mr. Perlman has been a phenomenal fiddler ever since he appeared on the scene about ten years ago, but he now has taken the quantum leap into a tiny group of artists ... who make audiences fall deeply in love with them."

The following year, Robert Sherman, in the same newspaper, also noted Itzhak's ever-deepening joy in music. "Itzhak Perlman can hardly be considered a musical elder statesman, having only last year turned the corner into his thirty's, but the Israeli violinist certainly played like one at Carnegie Hall .... Ease, elegance, assurance, and impeccable taste were prime elements in his approach along with the technical mastery ... even his posture and facial expressions echoed the joy that pervades his music making."

Music critic Peter Davis summed up Itzhak Perlman's triumph as a violinist. "He seems to have just about everything," Davis wrote, "a fabulous technique, a string sound of ravishing tonal properties, a warm romantic temperament ... a thoughtful musical intelligence and an indefinable personal aura that makes audiences love him."

Not only critics and audiences were dazzled by Itzhak's playing. Other virtuoso violinists were equally impressed, which is rare among musicians. His friend and mentor, Isaac Stern, who has himself sometimes been called the outstanding violinist of the twentieth century, describes Itzhak's talent as limitless. "Nobody comes anywhere near him in what he can physically do with the violin. He plays with incredible accuracy and dexterity." Other violinists have echoed Stern's comments.

Becoming successful is never enough for a true artist, or for anyone in any field of endeavor who sincerely cares about what he or she is doing. There are always deeper places to go, more complex problems to solve, additional concepts to learn, new avenues to explore. In the early years, Itzhak was most comfortable playing what musicians call the Romantic and virtuoso repertoires, meaning works by a composer such as Tchaikovsky. As the years went by, he began to deal with the challenges posed by the more classical composers. Itzhak himself described it. "You can tell your age by the repertory you are asked to play. At nineteen, I had Paganini, Tchaikovsky, Wieniawski coming out of my ears. Now I play Mozart, Beethoven, Brahms, Bartok, Stravinsky." With his penchant for joking, he couldn't help adding, "I'm getting old!" He found expanding into these deeper works to be more challenging. "It's just you and the music," Itzhak reported. "Timing and pacing are much more critical." Interpreting the music that the master composer Beethoven wrote in his later years is, according to Itzhak Perlman, "like learning a new language." In talking about these great pieces, he said, "The more you play them, the more you see in them."

Itzhak has never stopped working with ceaseless determination to learn all the languages of his chosen musical medium, the violin. "If I start saying, 'I'm at the top,' then I might as well quit," he pointed out, "because where can I go from there? What I think about is that I have a responsibility to keep on growing musically." In a 1988 interview, he was still saying, "I'm always in the process of learning new things."

Musicians, just like artists or writers or actors, have their own individual styles, which usually take time to be discovered and developed. Rock musicians often record a new song one way the first time. Then, several years later, it may be played quite differently on another album.

Itzhak's methods and techniques have changed through the years. It took work and concentration to develop his own unique style. He worked hard and listened to the criticism of his teachers and other musicians whose opinion he respected. At first, like most young soloists, he tended to imitate those who had preceded him. "There was the Heifetz period," he said, "when I used a lot of fast vibrato and fast tempi; the Oistrakh period, when I tried wide vibrato and sensuous rich tone, and the Stern period—when I didn't vibrate for a whole year."

The time came, however, when Itzhak's playing was no longer like anyone else's, and he found his own distinctive style of performance. The Perlman style has been described as one that "bares his soul" and that somehow sweeps his listeners into sharing his own personal experience with the music he is playing.

Itzhak also expanded his horizons by forming professional and personal relationships with other performers. Pinchas Zukerman, also Israeli-born, is a violinist with whom Itzhak played frequently. The two also became close personal friends. In 1975, Itzhak and

"Pinky," as Zukerman is nicknamed, traveled together throughout Europe. There, they not only performed in concert, but recorded and videotaped their violin duos. The twin virtuosos got along exceedingly well. "The formality just goes out the window," Itzhak said, expressing his pleasure. "Especially with Pinky, we know exactly what each one wants to do. We do it on the spur of the moment."

Itzhak also formed a partnership with pianist Vladimir Ashkenazy. He discovered that when they worked together, his own playing gained an extra dimension. It is no coincidence that both musicians are perfectionists. They worked on one Beethoven sonata for two and a half years before they were satisfied enough with the level of performance and interpretation. Only then were they willing to record it.

It is said that a workman is only as good as his tool. This may not be completely true for musicians, but even a virtuoso is limited in what he or she can accomplish with an inferior instrument. Once Itzhak became successful financially, he could now consider acquiring a fine violin. This is not as simple as it sounds. One doesn't just rush into a store and exclaim, "Give me a Stradivarius!" or "Do you have any good Guarneriuses in stock?" A musician doesn't put out hundreds of thousands of dollars for a violin every day. It must be selected cautiously. Any prospective instrument has to be tested with great care by the player who will use it to determine if it is exactly right for that person's style and technique. Finding the right violin can be as difficult as finding the right mate.

Itzhak Perlman searched for three years before he found the violin that was meant for him. Once he located his special Stradivarius, however, it was as though performer and instrument merged and became one. From then on, this instrument, created in the year

1714 by Antonio Stradivari, was the violin on which he would always perform.

There have been many high points in Itzhak's musical career. But strange events, too, seem to be drawn to him as nails are to a magnet. The newspaper strike after his Carnegie Hall debut and the theft of the Juilliard Guarnerius during the Leventritt Competition were not the only mysterious happenings to occur. On March 4, 1973, Itzhak was scheduled to give a recital in the Rogers Auditorium of the Metropolitan Museum of Art in New York City. That afternoon, the Museum received an anonymous telephone call. The caller threatened to assassinate the violinist, although no reason was given. There was a lot of excited talk and nervous suggestions to cancel the concert. It seemed the prudent thing to do. But Itzhak refused even to consider such action. The recital went on as scheduled, the only interference being that it was delayed a half hour while security guards carefully combed the area. Once begun, the concert proceeded smoothly. The violinist performed with his usual skill and with apparent disregard of any danger.

There have been many memorable moments in Itzhak's career. One such special event occurred the day after Thanksgiving in 1977. Itzhak honored his teacher, Ivan Galamian, on the occasion of the famed master's seventy-fifth birthday, by giving a gala party at the Perlmans' New York City apartment. Invited to the festivities were all of Galamian's students and former students who were still in the area. They came to pay homage to the old man. Many of Galamian's students, like Itzhak himself, were now accomplished artists. It was said that the guest list was like a "Who's Who" of violinists. The old master died only four years later.

Another highlight came on November 7, 1988, when Itzhak Perlman performed at the White House in

Washington, D.C. before President and Mrs. Reagan. He was opening the second season of a television series, "In Performance at the White House." The concert took place in the East Room, an ornate cream and gold room dominated by portraits of George and Martha Washington. Itzhak introduced one of his protégés, a young pianist named Ken Noda, and they performed several piano and violin duets together. President Reagan praised Itzhak for his musicianship and enthusiasm, saying that he had "the ebullience of a newly elected Congressman." This was actually Itzhak's third White House concert. He had also played for two previous presidents, Jimmy Carter and Richard Nixon.

On Wednesday, September 26, 1990, Itzhak was the star performer at an historic event. Carnegie Hall was celebrating the beginning of its one hundredth year. Outside the great temple of music in New York City, huge searchlights bathed the entering guests in a brilliant light. It was the legendary hall's Centennial Gala Opening Night. Together with Andre Previn and the Los Angeles Philharmonic, Itzhak treated the specially invited, formally attired audience to a concert featuring works by Beethoven, Barber, and Schumann. Unlike Itzhak's first performance at Carnegie Hall, which went unreported because of the newspaper strike, this landmark program was fully covered by the media with all the details appropriate to its importance in the world of music.

This was quite a contrast to that evening twenty-seven years previously when the nervous seventeen-year-old boy had made his debut here. Itzhak Perlman had reached the top of his profession. The disabled prodigy from Israel had become a superstar.

Chapter Nine

HIS PERSONAL LIFE

Itzhak Perlman's life has centered upon music. From the time he was a toddler in Israel, yearning to play like his idol, Jascha Heifetz, he dedicated himself to his instrument. The intricacies of violin performance dominated every aspect of his existence.

It seemed unlikely that anything could ever take precedence over music and musicians in Itzhak Perlman's special world. But something else began to grow in relevance and intensity as the years went by. Eventually, one thing and one thing alone became even more important to him than his beloved violin, and that was his family—his wife and his children. Itzhak's mother, Shoshana, died, and some time later, his father decided to return to Israel. This made Itzhak's immediate family even more precious and necessary to his happiness. His family became the rock that centered him to real life and to human relationships.

Toby Friedlander Perlman continued to remain as awed by her husband's incredible talent as she was on that summer day in 1963 at Meadowmount when she first heard him play and immediately determined that this maker of musical magic was the man she was going to marry. Time only deepened Toby's appreciation of Itzhak's ability. Her single-minded devotion to his talent and his career never wavered. She herself had received the finest classical music training as a student at Juilliard. She was an accomplished violinist in her own right. Early in their marriage, however, Toby Perlman decided that supporting and encouraging her husband's rare and unique gift was more important than pursuing a career of her own.

A little more than a year after their 1967 marriage, Itzhak and Toby Perlman were blessed with a son. They named him Noah. Two years later, their eldest daughter, Navah Miriam, was born. Navah was followed, four years later, by another girl, Leora. The Perlmans were now a family of five. Toby loved motherhood, and in 1980, she gave birth to another baby boy to whom they gave the name Rami. Several years later, their last child and youngest girl arrived on the scene. They called her Ariella, which means "little song."

Itzhak himself had been an only child. But his own household soon became a large, busy, and noisy one, and he was entranced by all the happy commotion. His career as a concert violinist involved a lot of travel away from home. More and more tours, both domestic and foreign, became necessary as his public fame grew. Itzhak was determined, however, to provide a normal life for his family, and he made a strong effort to spend as much time as possible with them. "I don't want to wake up one morning," he said, "and find that my children have grown up while I was on the road."

Itzhak intended to be a father who was there for his children when they needed him. He didn't want to miss all the events and occasions, both large and small, that dot and illuminate the growing-up years. He made it a practice, for example, never to accept a concert engagement on any of his children's birthdays. As

Itzhak and Toby Perlman with their daughter Ariella in their Manhattan home. (Photo courtesy of Sara Krulwich, NYT Pictures.)

his career flourished, it was sometimes necessary for him to spend long periods on the road. But even this hectic schedule could not keep him from his family. As much as possible, he managed to commute home in between concerts, even if it meant frequent flying back and forth.

Toby was the glue that kept the family together

and functioning. Their long-time friend, Isaac Stern, has described her as "God's gift" to Itzhak. She happily assumed the role of wife and mother in a way that many people would consider to be "old-fashioned." She watched carefully over her family's health and welfare, and involved herself deeply in her children's education, development, and growth. She once defined herself, in all seriousness, as a "nineteenth century wife and mother," adding, "maybe that's why our marriage works."

It did work, despite the increasing pressures that budding fame puts on the life of any family. Itzhak arranged his schedules so that even with his frequent absences, he continued to play an important role in his children's world. And Toby skillfully stepped in to fill any temporary gaps. Almost all of Itzhak's time, when not performing, was spent in the large, spacious apartment on the upper west side of Manhattan into which he and Toby had moved in the early years of their marriage. This home was the family's private castle. It was a fortress, protecting them from being disturbed by the press or public. Within these walls, Itzhak was not the glittering, formally-attired star of television and concert halls, but merely "Dad." Both parents encouraged the children to have neighborhood friends, to do well in school, and to pursue their individual interests.

Not surprisingly, the younger generation of Perlmans showed musical tendencies at an early age, especially Navah. Their eldest daughter seemed to have a special talent for the piano. Itzhak is proud of all his children and deeply interested in their accomplishments and problems. "If you're not careful," he once said, "the children will grow up on you and you'll miss the most glorious part of life." Itzhak has worked hard to make sure that this would never happen to him.

Sons and daughters of stars are often allowed to grow up without a strong, guiding parental presence.

Newspapers, magazines, and books, even talk shows, have described the special psychological problems that many of these young people seem to have. They are raised in affluence and given everything a child could want except a stable home life and the time and attention of their parents, which is what they desire the most. Aware of this danger, Toby Perlman guided her family ship with a strong rudder, making certain it followed a straight and clear course. Both she and Itzhak believed in loving but firm discipline, with reasonable but strict rules. Television watching was discouraged; homework time was carefully supervised. The children were encouraged to develop a sense of responsibility while still young by being given chores such as making their own beds or doing the dishes.

The Perlmans tried, as much as possible, to shelter their family from the disturbing glare of publicity. Their five children were brought up quietly. Their comings and goings were kept outside the limelight. The joys and challenges of rearing youngsters remained private, within the Perlman family. Very few people outside a small circle of relatives and friends knew, for example, that the eldest son, Noah, developed a severe case of juvenile rheumatoid arthritis when he was eight years old. From that time, until the age of eleven, Noah had to use a wheelchair to get around. This, like most other issues involving the children, was considered a family matter. It was certainly not something to be exposed to the curiosity and examination of strangers.

It was not easy for a famous performer like Itzhak Perlman to raise his children in a secure, normal atmosphere. With Toby's unfailing support, however, this was somehow accomplished. The children grew up in an environment that did not seem very different from the average, upper-middle class homes of their friends.

There were, to be sure, some small but significant differences. For example, visitors to the Perlman apartment tended to be somewhat unlike average guests elsewhere. Well-known people such as violinists Isaac Stern and Pinchas Zukerman, conductor Zubin Mehta, and other musicians were an everyday part of the Perlman children's special world. This seemed unremarkable and perfectly normal to them.

The Perlmans longed for even greater privacy than was possible in the city. In 1980 they bought a secluded country home near a lake in upstate New York. It was a perfect place for the children to romp and play freely in the fresh mountain air, and for Itzhak to unwind on weekends between stressful tours. The lake house soon became very special to the Perlmans. They even gave it a name—"Ritardando." This is a musical term that means "slowing down," and that is exactly what Itzhak was able to do there.

In many ways, Ritardando was a typical lakeshore home. It was a simple shingle building with a main loft-like living space that included a living room, dining area, and large kitchen. The house was, however, given some special and unique features. It was remodeled in order to adapt it to the needs of a handicapped resident. For example, all the doorways were enlarged to a width of thirty-six inches. This allowed enough space for a wheelchair to pass through smoothly. Originally there were steps that led from the garage to the kitchen. These were replaced with a ramp, also meant to accommodate a wheelchair. An electric chairlift was installed on the inner staircase to provide easy travel up and down. Even some of the furniture was designed to suit the disabled. Chairs were constructed with the seats higher than usual. The custom-made bed in the master bedroom had long drawers built in underneath the mattress. This was handy for storing crutches at night.

Most important of all, however, this country home was a place where the Perlman family was able to be together far away from the demands and tensions of Itzhak's brilliant but demanding career. Here, he was able to find release from the pressures on Itzhak Perlman, the superstar of concert stage and media. Here, he could be Itzhak Perlman, the husband and father, the devoted family man.

Most of the hobbies and interests that Itzhak developed outside of the violin tended to be family- or home-oriented. One of his most avid passions became food and food preparation. This interest began in the late 1960s, at a time when Itzhak feared that he was gaining too much weight. He put the blame for these extra pounds on the huge, rich restaurant meals he had been eating. Nothing, not even his disability, had ever before held Itzhak back from attempting something new. He saw no reason now why he shouldn't try to improve his diet by cooking for himself. The first cooking experiment he tried for his new low-calorie regime was with chicken. "I boiled the chicken ... and cooked it with V-8 juice," he recalled, adding with pride, "It was quite tasty."

He *fiddled* around in the kitchen (this is the sort of pun that Itzhak likes to inflict upon his friends) by himself for a while, experimenting and mixing ingredients like a scientist in a laboratory. Then, in an effort to improve his cooking skills, he sought advice and instruction. The average individual who is looking for advice on how to cook might consult his or her mom or grandmother or Uncle Joe, the outstanding chef of the family. That person might even enroll in a cooking class at the local community school. When Itzhak Perlman wanted to know more about this subject, however, it was star performer Danny Kaye and world-famous chef Virginia Lee who taught him the techniques of

Chinese cookery. Itzhak was especially fond of this type of food for several reasons, some of which arose from his sociable, gregarious nature. "With Chinese food, you need more people," he once explained. "You need variety; it's not food for when you're alone."

After that, Itzhak branched out into many different types of cookery. He had fun improvising and trying out new combinations in his role as an amateur chef. "I make do with what's in the refrigerator," he once commented. Using whatever was available, he liked to try reproducing interesting dishes he had tasted in restaurants. Itzhak found that he enjoyed puttering around in the kitchen and preparing family meals. Wearing an apron inscribed "Itzhak's Kitchen," he often made extra quantities of one of his specialties, meat loaf, for his family to eat while he was away on a tour. He was eager to share the secrets of the Perlman meat loaf method with a *New York Times* interviewer: "The important thing about this is to sauté the onions and then the garlic before you put them into the meat," he confided. "The more breadcrumbs you use, the better it tastes."

Itzhak's love of cooking may stem from the fact that, unlike playing the violin, cooking doesn't require a lot of practice. As a violinist, he must master exacting and difficult techniques. As a cook, however, he can express himself freely and with abandon. "It was instant gratification," was how he described his enjoyment of cooking. Sautéing onions and tossing in spices and herbs are not quite the same as ploughing through the intricacies of a complex and technically challenging sonata.

Acquiring fresh skills can often cause new doors to open. Itzhak's love of food and cooking created some interesting situations for him. In addition to being a guest on public television's "The Frugal Gourmet," he once participated in a commercial for Sara Lee croissants.

One of Itzhak's other enthusiasms is sports. He had gradually developed into an avid sports fan, becoming widely known for his loud support of New York teams such as the Yankees and the Knicks. He and Toby attend baseball and basketball games as much as his busy schedule will permit. He is especially passionate about baseball, and so he was doubly enthralled by the fact that their New York apartment was once occupied by the legendary Babe Ruth. His enthusiasm for baseball even spilled into the concert arena. Once, when performing in Kansas with pianist Samuel Sanders, Itzhak brought onto the stage Dan Quisenberry, who was then the star relief pitcher of the Kansas City Royals. Quisenberry presented the two musicians with autographed baseballs inscribed, "My best to the best." Since both Itzhak and the pianist considered themselves to be two of the hottest baseball fans in the country, the pitcher's appearance on stage with them was a real thrill. At a reception later, most of the talk was not about music, but about the past baseball season, much to Itzhak's delight. After all, he approaches his hobbies and interests with the same verve and enthusiasm that brought him stardom as a classical musician.

Chapter Ten

A SPOKESMAN FOR THE DISABLED

Many of the children who attend Public School 199 in New York City are disabled. Some of them can only get around in wheelchairs or with the aid of crutches.

In March of 1977, the students of P.S. 199 put on a show. It was a program of songs from around the world. The children performed, wore costumes, and painted scenery. They did all the usual things that are necessary to produce a show. Some of the guests who attended were amazed that "disabled" children could accomplish so much. Those who knew these boys and girls best, however, were not at all surprised. Their parents, teachers, counselors, and friends were accustomed to looking upon them as persons first, disabled second. "People have a hard time seeing a kid in a wheelchair as normal," one of their teachers explained, adding, "They're bright! They're lively. They're normal!"

The children themselves knew what they were capable of, but they were also well aware of negative public attitudes toward the handicapped. "When people meet us, they think we don't know anything," one girl complained. "They're up-tight. They treat us like babies."

There was one guest at that show who wasn't the

Itzhak Perlman entertaining young patients at Strong Memorial Hospital in Rochester, New York. (Photo courtesy of Gannett Rochester Newspapers.)

least bit "up-tight" about the young performers or astonished at their accomplishments. Like them, he got around only with the aid of crutches or a wheelchair. This had never held him back from achievement, and he saw no reason why these boys and girls should be limited either. That guest was Itzhak Perlman. He beamed with pride at the accomplishments of the students. He had entertained them himself only a short time earlier. His relaxed attitude about his own disabilities helped to build up their confidence. Not only did he play the violin for them but he also joked around. He "played" on one of his crutches as though it was a flute, and even pretended to eat his Stradivarius. The boys and girls loved it. The carefree, lighthearted way in which he treated his handicap somehow made theirs seem more manageable. "He acted like a comedian!" exclaimed one of the laughing children.

Itzhak didn't talk down to the students nor did he downplay the difficulties of being disabled. He frankly admitted what they all knew — that many people do look at them differently and that sometimes this can be hard to take. But he also emphasized how important it was for them to know what their own individual aspirations were and then to go ahead and reach for these goals. "The most difficult thing," he told the children, "is not the difficulty itself, but society's attitude towards it."

Itzhak Perlman has worked tirelessly to change that particular attitude. Acting as a positive role model for disabled children is only one of the ways he has tried to make life easier for the handicapped. His appearance at P.S. 199 is one of many visits he has made to schools and hospitals, speaking to youngsters with disabilities. Bringing a sense of play and lightness into their lives, he has played for them, kidded around a lot, and encouraged the boys and girls to participate.

Once, when visiting Blythedale Children's Hospital in New York state, he took his bow apart and showed the children how it was made out of horsehair. "Obviously," he joked, "it came from Secretariat." (Secretariat was a champion racehorse that had won so many races his name was familiar to everyone at the time.) On this same visit, Itzhak delighted the boys and girls by coaxing mooing and twittering sounds from his instrument. He then encouraged the children to sing their favorite songs and cheerfully provided accompaniment for them on his violin.

Itzhak has been a spokesman for the disabled in other ways too. After all, he knows from personal experience the obstacles that face a handicapped person in a world constructed for those without disabilities. His particular career involves much traveling and movement from place to place. The life of a concert performer can be physically difficult and tiring even for those without handicaps. Yet Itzhak Perlman flies around the world and manages to get from airport to hotel to concert halls in taxis and on his crutches. When performing or rehearsing in the New York area, he even drives himself around in his own Volvo, which is specially equipped with hand controls.

In his journeys around the world, Itzhak Perlman has had to face countless numbers of hotels, airports, and concert stages that were unfriendly to a person on crutches or in a wheelchair. Although few people ever saw him frustrated or angry in those circumstances, he has expressed his feelings in many interviews and articles. "I've been in public buildings throughout the world," he once wrote, "and it's clear that the people who design them have no idea what it feels like to use crutches or sit in a wheelchair."

As an example of the worst possible design from the point of view of a concertgoer, Itzhak mentions the

Sydney Opera House in Australia. He calls it an "architectural catastrophe." This particular building's design came about as the result of a contest. The prize-winning architect created a gorgeous, impressive structure. It was made even more grand by the steep, imposing flight of stairs that lead up to the entrance. The designer probably thought that even an elevator might spoil the beautiful symmetry of the design, because none was installed. Everyone entering the building has to climb up those daunting steps. Any members of the public who are frail, elderly, or disabled are, therefore, effectively barred from enjoying concerts in this hall. As for the musicians themselves, even those with no handicaps have difficulty lugging their heavy instruments up the stairs. Imagine what a trial it is for performers, like Itzhak Perlman, who have to deal with disabilities.

"Why couldn't the prize have been given to the best design that was also barrier-free?" Itzhak asked indignantly. "Why, when it's possible to make everyone comfortable, is so little attention paid to accessibility? It's mind-boggling!"

Itzhak Perlman has done all he can to change this indifference to the needs of the handicapped by the designers of public buildings. "I spend hours on long-distance phone calls," he once said, "telling architects about how to design barrier-free buildings." As a superstar of the classical concert world, Itzhak found that when he refused to play in some halls because of access problems, these difficulties were quickly remedied—creating new possibilities not only for the performer, but for those in the audience who are disabled as well.

Itzhak worked closely with the architect who designed the remodeling of his country house in upstate New York. Many special details were included to make the house convenient and safe for his use. Wide doorways were installed for the use of a wheelchair. The wood tile floors were deliberately set in unevenly. The purpose of this type of floor construction is to provide traction. A smoothly-sanded floor can be dangerous to someone who is using crutches.

Through Itzhak Perlman's efforts, more building designers have become sensitive to the needs of the handicapped. He has lectured to architects around the world, trying to help them see the usefulness of what he calls "universal designs," which can accommodate everyone, disabled and non-disabled alike. I.M. Pei, who is one of the top architects in the world, is one of those who are impressed with Itzhak's ideas. "Mr. Perlman has dramatized many important points for me," Pei said, "and together we are working on some exciting new ideas to enable disabled people not only to be comfortable using a building, but to truly enjoy it as well." Together with sympathetic architects, Itzhak has tried to see to it that every disabled person could enter any concert hall in the country with the same ease as a non-disabled person. "Personally," he remarked with a wry grin, "I never want to have to take the garbage elevator to get to the stage."

A lot has been accomplished, much of it due at least partially to Itzhak Perlman's efforts. But big hurdles still exist. In April 1990 Itzhak performed in a benefit concert at the Garde Arts Center in New London, Connecticut. He also gave advice to the members of a committee who were working on plans to restore the old concert hall. Itzhak told the committee how upset he always becomes when theaters build a special "Perlman ramp" for his performance, then remove it the next day. "This is missing the point," he insisted to the committee. "The audience needs to use this as much as the performer."

Concert halls are not the only target of Itzhak Perlman's crusade to make the world more accessible for the disabled. He has pointed out the problems that handicapped people encounter with airport travel and hotels, and how simply and inexpensively some of these difficulties could be solved. Once he described a hotel he stayed at in Israel where there were five steps that led down to the pool. He pointed out this inconvenience to the manager, who immediately installed a ramp alongside the steps. Itzhak was amused to notice that, once installed, the ramp was not used by the handicapped alone. "Nine out of ten people used the ramp, not the steps," he remarked. "They preferred the ramp whether they needed it or not."

Itzhak has also done all in his power to educate the public to the fact that someone with a disability is a human being first and foremost. Everyone living is plagued by problems of one sort or another. A disabled person's handicap is just his particular problem. It is something he has to learn to adjust to, but it doesn't change all other aspects of his personality, spirit, and capabilities.

Itzhak has always played down the problems that his own handicap has posed to him as a performer. He says that walking onto a stage with crutches has always been normal for him. It is something he has done all his life. It is, however, far from simple. Most people do not realize the numerous details that must be given careful attention just for him to get ready to perform.

First of all, once on stage he must maneuver himself from a standing position onto the chair where he will sit. The casualness with which he does this carefully disguises the fact that one false move or miscalculation could be disastrous. The chair must be positioned perfectly. His crutches must be aligned correctly. His feet have to be pointed exactly. A misstep could easily lead to a dangerous and embarrassing fall. Of course, he cannot execute this tricky maneuver while holding a violin, so someone else must bring his instrument to him after he has been seated. The whole procedure gets even trickier when he plays with an orchestra. Then, his chair is placed upon a podium (a raised area). This means an additional step up to overcome. Finally, he stores his crutches beneath his chair and is ready to begin.

Difficult as this prelude to performing seems, the challenge after the concert looms even larger. First, Itzhak must hand his precious Stradivarius to his accompanist or to the concertmaster. Then he drags out his crutches from under the chair. Using them for support, he must pull himself up, using only the strength of his arms, and transfer his entire weight of two hundred pounds onto the crutches. He makes the procedure look effortless and has even joked about it, commenting, "I feel like a champion weight lifter." It is not easy at all. Only Itzhak's cheerful, accepting attitude makes it seem so.

Concert stages are only one of the challenges Itzhak has learned to handle in his encounter with the outside world. Itzhak often relates the story of his experience in an airport when he was sitting in a wheelchair. The clerk behind the check-in counter refused to look at Itzhak. He kept staring past him, directing his remarks to Itzhak's companion. "When's his flight?" the clerk inquired. "Where's he going?" It wasn't until Itzhak declared, "Look, you can ask *me* all those questions. I'm perfectly capable of answering," that the clerk would speak directly to him. "When able-bodied people see someone in a wheelchair," Itzhak once wrote, "they assume that if he or she can't walk, the person can't do anything — like hear, talk, or think." Itzhak Perlman has tried to change all that, partly by his own example, and partly by speaking out wherever and whenever possible to change the public's perception of disabilities.

Itzhak Perlman has championed the cause of the disabled in every way that he can. He was a member of the United Nations Committee for the International Year of Disabled Persons. He served on the board of directors of the Blythedale Children's Hospital, in Valhalla, New York, and on the President's Committee for the Employment of the Handicapped. He has written articles. He has appeared on television and before many groups, and he has used his influence as a respected and admired musical artist to dramatize the needs of the handicapped. Even when he appeared at the White House in Washington in 1982 to perform for President Reagan, he managed to bring his favorite crusade into the discussion, boldly mentioning the "terrible cuts" that the Reagan administration had attempted to make in federal programs to aid the handicapped.

Mostly, however, it is by his own example that Itzhak Perlman demonstrates that a human being does not have to be defined by his disability. His musical gifts bring joy to millions of music lovers around the world. His cheerful, outgoing personality and willingness to display both his handicap and his art before the mass media influence even more members of the public in understanding the two areas that are the most important to him. The huge, worldwide audience is able to see clearly that even a major handicap does not have to keep someone from achieving his heart's desire. And more and more people of all ages, in all locations, have come to know and enjoy classical music. "The greatest compliment that anyone can give me after a concert," Itzhak told an interviewer, "is to say, 'Gee, this is my first classical concert, and I really enjoyed it!'"

Itzhak Perlman has received many honors and awards as an artist and as a humanitarian. One that combined both these aspects of his life was given to him by the Medical University of South Carolina in Charleston. Along with Dr. Albert Sabin, who had developed the oral polio vaccine in the early 1960s, Itzhak was granted an honorary medical degree. His citation read, "To a careworn world, you are a refreshing spirit of courage and joy. You have transformed music into a healing art among nations."

BIBLIOGRAPHY

Ballantine, Bill, *The Violin*. New York: Franklin Watts, 1971.

Bowles, Jerry, *A Thousand Sundays*. New York: Putnam, 1980.

Campbell, Margaret, *The Great Violinists*. New York: Doubleday & Co., 1980.

Cron, Theodore O. and Goldblatt, Burt, *Portrait of Carnegie Hall*. New York: Macmillan, 1966.

Schickel, Richard, *The World of Carnegie Hall*. New York: Julian Messner, 1960.

Schwarz, Boris, *Great Masters of the Violin*. New York: Simon & Schuster, 1982.

INDEX

A
Abel, David, 73
Adademy of Music, Tel Aviv, 12, 47, 49
Allen, Peter, 66
Amati, Andreas, 38
Amati, Antonio, 38
Amati, Hieronymus, 38
Amati, Nicola, 38
America-Israel Cultural Foundation, 49, 59, 60, 61
America-Israel Culture House, 86
Armstrong, Louis, 66
Ashkenazy, Vladimir, 99

B
Bach, Johann Sebastian, 73
Barber, Samuel, 101
Barrier-free buildings, 117-8
Bartok, Bela, 97
Beatles, 54
Beethoven, Ludwig von, 97, 99, 101
Bender, William, 74, 80
Bennett, John, 68
Bernstein, Leonard, 51
Biancolli, Louis, 80
Bogart, Humphrey, 54
Brahms, Johannes, 97
Bris, 20
Broadcasting Orchestra, 50

C
Callas, Maria, 54

"Caravan of Stars," see "Ed Sullivan Caravan of Stars"
Carmen, 21
Carnegie Hall, 12, 59, 64, 65-70, 73, 79, 94, 96, 100, 101
Carter, Jimmy, 101
Castleman, Charles, 73
Chicago Daily News, 80
Chung, Kyung-Wha, 62
Churchill, Winston, 66
Circumcision, 20
Cultural Center of Tel Aviv, 32

D
Davis, Peter, 96-7
DeLay, Dorothy, 60-1, 62-3
Denver, John, 93
"Different Kind of Blues, A," 94
Disabled, Itzhak Perlman speaks out for the, 113-22

E
"Ed Sullivan Caravan of Stars, The," 12, 55-7
"Ed Sullivan Show, The," 53-6, 63, 79, 91
Ellington, Duke, 66

F
"Flight of the Bumblebee," 56
Fonteyn, Margot, 54
Foss, Lukas, 73
Frederic R. Mann Auditorium, 32, 48, 84

Fried, Miriam, 62
Friedlander, Mr. and Mrs. Harold, 86
Friedlander, Toby, see Perlman, Toby
"Frugal Gourmet, The," 91, 110-1

G

Galamian, Ivan, 12, 61-3, 81, 100
Garland, Judy, 66
Goldberg, Albert, 89
Goldcart, Madame Rivka, 49
Goodman, Benny, 66
Great Masters of the Violin, 123
Great Violinists, The, 123
Guarneri, Joseph, 38
Guarnerius violin, 75-6, 99
Guthrie, Arlo, 66

H

Haaretz, 84
"Habimah," 32
Hall, Jim, 94
Heifetz, Jascha, 21, 33, 42, 80, 81, 98, 103
Helena Rubinstein Museum of Arts, 32
Henahan, Donal J., 80, 92, 96
Herald Tribune, 90
Hope, Bob, 54
Hume, Paul, 76
Hurok, Sol, 70, 79, 83, 89

I

Infantile paralysis, 22
International Edgar M. Levenritt Contest, 70-7, 79, 86, 100
Israel National Youth Symhony Orchestra, 79-80

Israel Philharmonic Orchestra, 32, 48, 84

J

Joplin, Scott, 94
Juilliard School, 60-4, 75, 76, 81, 82, 86

K

Katherine Tuck Fund, 61
Kaye, Danny, 109
Kenny, Sister Elizabeth, 28, 29
  photo, 29
Kibbutz, 17
Kosher, 20, 57

L

Lee, Virginia, 109-10
Leventritt, Edgar, 71
Leventritt competition, see International Edgar M. Leventritt Contest
Leventritt Foundation, 70
Liszt, Franz, 43
Los Angeles Philharmonic, 101
Los Angeles Times, 89
Lowens, Irving, 76
Lyre, 36

M

Mann, Shelly, 94
Meadowmount, 81-3, 86, 103
Mehta, Zubin, 108
Mendelssohn, Felix, 56
Menuhin, Yehudi, 70
Mitchell, Red, 94
Mozart, Wolfgang Amadeus, 73, 97

N

National Orchestral Association, 63

National Symphony Orchestra, 76, 79
New York Herald Tribune, 74, 80
New York Philharmonic Orchestra, 85, 89
New York Times, 76, 85, 90, 96, 110
New York World Telegram, 80
Nishizaki, Takako, 73
Nixon, Richard, 101
Noda, Ken, 101
Nureyev, Rudolf, 54
Nutcracker, The, 67

P

Paganini, Niccolo, 42-3, 97
Pavarotti, Luciano, 93
Pei, I.M., 118
Perlman, Ariella, 104, 105
  photo, 105
Perlman, Chaim, 16-7, 20-5, 27-8, 31-3, 45-6, 50-1, 55-6, 57-9, 86, 103
  handling Itzhak's disability, 45-6, 50-1
  returns to Israel, 103
Perlman, Itzhak, 11-122
  attends Juilliard, 60-4, 81
  birth, 20
  Caravan of Stars, 55-7
  Carnegie Hall debut, 65-70
  childhood, 45-51
  children, 87, 104-7
  contracts polio, 24-5
  cooking, 92, 109-11
  courtship, 82-3, 85
  expanding musical horizons, 89-101
  fights back from polio, 27-33

Perlman, Itzhak, cont.
  handling his disability, 47-8, 50
  honors and awards, 122
  jokes, 92, 109
  learning to play the violin, 21, 32-3, 43-4, 46-7, 49-50
  Leventritt contest, 72-7
  personal life, 103-11
  photos, 72, 94, 105, 114
  spokesman for the disabled, 113-22
  strange luck, 69-70, 74-6, 100
  t.v. appearances, 91, 93, 95
Perlman, Leora, 104
Perlman, Navah Miriam, 104, 106
Perlman, Noah, 104, 107
Perlman, Rami, 104
Perlman, Shoshana, 16-7, 20-5, 27-8, 31-3, 45-6, 50-1, 56, 57-9, 75, 86, 103
  death, 103
  handling Itzhak's disability, 45-6, 50-1
Perlman, Toby, 81-3, 85, 86-7, 103-11
  children, 87, 104-7
  courtship, 81-3, 85
  marriage, 86-7
  photo, 105
Peters, Roberta, 54
Philharmonic Orchestra, Israeli, 32, 48
"Pineapple Rag," 94
Polio, 12, 13, 22-5, 27-33
  rehabilitation, 27-33
  Sister Kenny's methods of treating, 28-30
  treatment, photos, 29

Poliomyelitis, see Polio
"Polonaise Brillante," 56
Portrait of Carnegie Hall, 123
Presley, Elvis, 54
Previn, Andre, 94, 101

R

Ramat-Gan Orchestra of Tel Aviv, 49
Ravel, Maurice, 82
Reagan, Ronald, 101, 121
Rimsky-Korsakov, Nicolai, 56
"Ritardando," 108-9, 117-8
Rogers Auditorium, 100
Rolling Stones, 66
Roosevelt, Theodore, 66
Ruth, Babe, 87, 111

S

Sabin, Albert, 22, 122
Sabras, 49
Salk, Jonas, 22
Sanders, Samuel, 111
Schumann, Robert, 101
"Sesame Street," 91, 93, 94
  photo, 94
Sherman, Robert, 96
Sibelius, Jean, 80, 84
"60 Minutes," 91, 92
Sleeping Beauty, 67
Soltis, Rabbi Avraham, 86
Stern, Isaac, 51, 58, 59, 60, 70, 96, 97, 98, 106, 108
  photo, 58
Stradivari, Antonio, 38, 100
Stradivarius violin, 11, 37, 46, 99, 115, 120
  photo, 37
Stravinsky, Igor, 97
Sullivan, Ed, 12, 51, 53-5

Szell, George, 73

T

Tchaikovsky, Peter Ilyitch, 67, 73, 79, 84, 97
Thousand Sundays, A, 123
"Tonight Show, The," 91
Tosca, 93
Traviata, La, 21
"Turkey in the Straw," 94
Tuthill, William Burnet, 66
"Tzigane," 82

V

Violin, 21, 35-44
  introduction to, 35-44
  parts of, 39, 40-1
  illustration, 39
Violin, The, 123

W

Wallace, Mike, 92
Washington, George and Martha, 101
Washington Evening Star, 76
Washington Post, 76-7
White House, 100-1, 121
Wieniawski, Henri, 56, 68, 73, 97
Wilson, Woodrow, 66
World of Carnegie Hall, The, 123

Y

Youth Symphony of New York, 63

Z

Zionist Organization of America, 59, 60
Zukerman, Pinchas, 62, 98-9, 108